Writing Myths

Applying Second Language Research to Classroom Teaching

JOY REID

with Keith S. Folse
Cynthia M. Schuemann
Pat Byrd and John Bunting
Ken Hyland
Dana Ferris
Susan Conrad
Sharon Cavusgil
Paul Kei Matsuda

Ann Arbor
University of Michigan

ISBN-13: 978-0-472-03257-0

2011   2010   2009   2008   4   3   2   1

Contents

Introduction   v

Myth 1   Teaching Vocabulary Is Not the Writing Teacher's Job   1
Keith S. Folse, University of Central Florida

Myth 2   Teaching Citation Is Someone Else's Job   18
Cynthia M. Schuemann, Miami Dade College

Myth 3   Where Grammar Is Concerned, One Size Fits All   42
Pat Byrd and John Bunting, Georgia State University

Myth 4   Make Your Academic Writing Assertive and Certain   70
Ken Hyland, University of London

Myth 5   Students Must Learn to Correct All Their Writing Errors   90
Dana Ferris, California State University–Sacramento

Myth 6   Corpus-Based Research Is Too Complicated to
Be Useful for Writing Teachers   115
Susan Conrad, Portland State University

Myth 7   Academic Writing Courses Should Focus on
Paragraph and Essay Development   140
Sharon Cavusgil, Georgia State University

Myth 8   International and U.S. Resident ESL Writers Cannot
Be Taught in the Same Class   159
Paul Kei Matsuda, Arizona State University

Myth(s) 9   Students' Myths about Academic Writing
and Teaching   177
Joy Reid, Maui Community College

Author Biodata   202
Index   205

Introduction

WHEN I READ KEITH FOLSE'S *Vocabulary Myths: Applying Second Language Research to Classroom Teaching* (University of Michigan Press, 2004), I was impressed by the quality of the material but also, and especially, by its presentation. First, each myth is defined. Then, reasons why each myth is counter to good teaching practice are carefully explained, with the published research on which the explanation is based briefly summarized in a chart (for readers who wish to match up the research with the explanation). The final, extended section offers readers helpful pedagogy to substitute for the myth, including methods and materials, sample lesson plans, and specific assignments. Just as important, the chapters are written in a relatively informal way, with personal experiences, student examples, and even humor. Wow, I thought: ESL writing teachers need a similar resource.

Compared with my initial ESL teaching experiences that began 44 years ago, so many resources are now available for teachers, so much research has been reported, that there is even a *Journal of Second Language Writing*. Still, an easily accessible, even inviting and enjoyable book about "best practices" in writing classrooms interested me. Further, certain teaching myths have emerged over the years and, unfortunately, some have prevailed. Worse, writing teachers may be perpetuating those myths.

So I wrote Keith for permission to use his template, then contacted ESL composition specialists to ask them (a) which important writing myths they thought needed to be "outed" and replaced in the ESL writing classroom and (b) which they might choose to write about. Several colleagues agreed to write "myth" chapters that were based on their research and teaching experiences. The result is *Writing Myths: Applying Second Language Research to Classroom Teaching*.

Each author in this collection is a practicing teacher who selected his or her myth based on classroom experience and expertise. In the first section of the chapter, **In the Real World**, the teacher-author draws from his or her discovery of a writing myth by describing ways the myth is often used in writing classroom—and why it doesn't "work." Next, in **What the Research Says and Shows**, the author explains the foundation for eliminating the myth from the ESL writing classroom, including the causes and/or the effects of that myth on ESL writing—for both teaching and learning. The explanation is based on reported research that demonstrates the fallacy of the myth; the research is simply outlined in a chart—interested readers may consult the original research for additional information. The longer third section of each chapter, **What We Can Do,** provides multiple examples of classroom presentation and practice from the author's own repertoire, effectively giving readers materials for best practices that have proved successful in the ESL writing classroom.

Keith S. Folse (University of Central Florida) uses the first chapter to focus specifically on the myth that ESL writing classrooms are not the place to teach vocabulary. Cynthia M. Schuemann (Miami Dade College) follows with Myth 2—that teaching citation conventions isn't really a necessary part of the ESL writing curriculum. Next, Pat Byrd and John Bunting (Georgia State University) discuss why "One Grammar Fits All" is a myth, and Ken Hyland (University of London) confronts the myth that English academic writing should be definite, strong, assertive, even confrontative. Dana Ferris (California State University–Sacramento) takes on Myth 5, that students must learn to correct all their writing errors, while Susan Conrad (Portland State University) dispels the myth that corpus-discourse studies are too difficult to be included in ESL writing class curricula. Sharon Cavusgil (Georgia State University) argues that ESL academic writing classes must teach more than the paragraph and the essay, and Paul Matsuda (Arizona State University) discusses the reasons that ESL and resident students, despite their language learning differences, can be taught in the same classroom. At the end of the book, my chapter doesn't fit the template. Instead, I report on the myths students hold about composition instruction and instructors.

Both the research and the pedagogy in this book are based on the newest research in, for example, teacher preparation, EAP and ESP, and corpus linguistics. In fact, most of the chapters refer to and employ discourse analysis in the explanations. As a result, in the course of these chapters, other, often connected myths are raised and discussed. These include issues such as genre/disciplinary writing conventions, the essential reading-writing connection, teacher-responses to student writing, authenticity of writing assignments, and identifying and spiraling difficult writing tasks throughout the ESL writing curriculum.

Of course, other writing myths exist. Three others suggested by my initial survey are:

- thinking and planning writing in one's L1 is a bad idea
- non-standard English is lazy and must be fixed
- peer response/review groups are worthless

However, the chapters in this book focus on the most widespread myths that are currently being practiced in ESL writing courses. Further, issues that entire ESL/EFL resource books have already discussed (e.g., Generation 1.5 and grading issues) at length have been excluded. We hope that you will find our information helpful, that you will find the suggested methods and approaches effective, and that you will contact us with your questions and comments through the University of Michigan Press at *esladmin@umich.edu.*

1

Teaching Vocabulary Is Not the Writing Teacher's Job

Keith S. Folse
University of Central Florida

In the Real World

"NOT ANOTHER PLAGIARIZED PAPER," I thought to myself as I graded a set of academic research essays. The assignment in this particular case was to write an argumentative essay using information from at least two of three sources that we had read in class. The problem wasn't that the whole paper was plagiarized. In this paper, as in other students' papers, certain clauses or other large chunks of words had been lifted from the original readings and inserted into the student's paper. Examples: (a) *if we consider only these pertinent facts*, (b) *in judging the seriousness of their actions*, and (c) *a sharp rise in certain crimes has accompanied this unchecked population growth*. Since we had discussed plagiarism and cultural attitudes toward it at length, and I was sure that everyone in the class had understood our discussion, I found my anger growing with each plagiarized phrase.

On this student's paper and on the original articles, I highlighted with a yellow marker the dozen or so words/phrases that were identical.

1

Then, in a conference with the student, I showed him the highlighted areas. I asked him directly why he had plagiarized. Genuinely surprised by my question, the student answered, "I didn't plagiarize. I can't say these things in a better way. I think this is the best vocabulary to say this. Whatever I write isn't going to be as good."

The sincerity of this student made me stop to think. He was a good student. He had obviously spent time and effort on this assignment. His paper was rather good—except that he had taken language directly from the articles in more than a few cases. (I'm not justifying his actions, just explaining them.) The more I thought about what he had said about the limits of his vocabulary knowledge, the more I was inclined to agree with him: He couldn't express these ideas better than the original author had.

In fact, that was the problem. In a research writing assignment, the goal is not to copy the original author's information but to use the strategies of paraphrasing, summarizing, and synthesizing. Each of these strategies is complex and, at least in part, culturally based. Further, each requires both more than "using your own words" because, in reporting the ideas of others, precision is essential. Therefore, a paraphrase or summary will almost certainly use some terms—words and phrases—from the original. Even native speakers of English have difficulty writing academic summaries and paraphrases. For an ESL student who is a competent reader, who can distinguish the hierarchy of main ideas from specific detail, and who can make correct decisions about what material to use, questions still arise: which original terms should be used, and for which can a substitute synonym be used? The answers require (a) full understanding of the words and phrases in the original and (b) knowledge of another set of words and phrases to express those same ideas.

In other words, paraphrasing requires extensive vocabulary. The summary or paraphrase writer must not only be able to select the most precise original terms to use but also to express original ideas with alternate but accurate vocabulary at the same level of sophistication as the original. Further, the student writer must be familiar with a wide range of collocations. For instance, how would a non-native speaker (NNS) know that *sharp* collocates with *rise* (e.g., *a sharp rise in crime*) or that we don't say *important circumstances* or *urgent circumstances* but *dire circumstances*?

When I brought up this example in a teacher meeting, the ensuing discussion focused on the role of vocabulary in student writing. I pointed out that ESL students who recognize a phrase in an original text as "advanced English" and therefore native-like to them also understand (as my student has stated) that that phrase is "the best vocabulary to say this." In my experience, I said, what we call plagiarism may more often be a result of lexical limitations, even lexical ignorance and desperation, than cultural differences or outright cheating. I suggested that since, in this writing course, paraphrasing and summarizing were two important objectives, what was missing was appropriate directed vocabulary instruction to allow for proper paraphrasing and summarizing.

The discussion was diffuse and was interspersed with teachers' comments about the need for more grammar training. I argued that even though insufficient grammar won't block comprehension, insufficient vocabulary will certainly do so. For instance, when a student writes, *All people must waiting for the bus at the hot weather and when it is raining cats and dogs,* a native English speaker (NES) can understand the student's meaning. The writer's message is transparent despite three common grammatical errors, namely article omission *(all people* instead of *all the people),* modal phrase *(waiting* instead of *wait),* and incorrect preposition *(at* instead of *in).* In contrast, when an NNS writes, *The whole people must expect the bus in the hot weather and when there are cats and dogs,* the message is not transparent. In fact, most NESs would find it necessary to re-read this second sentence several times but still may not understand the writer's message. Although the three grammar mistakes in the first sentence may hinder comprehension, the writer's message is easy to understand; in the second sentence, the lexical errors *(The whole people,* and particularly the misuse of *cats and dogs)* make the sentence nearly incomprehensible. It is fair to say that grammatical errors are generally local, so they have small (but incremental) effects on readers, but they rarely blur the writer's intended message. In contrast, lexical errors often present larger, more global problems, creating a sort of domino effect as the reader attempts to use meaning obtained from incorrect vocabulary to decipher subsequent unclear words.

Finally, one teacher-voice said, "You know, I'm sure that vocabulary is important and all, but is this the writing teacher's job? We have *enough* to do." (Thus, although many students list "more vocabulary" as very important in their ESL learning, the myth believed by many teachers is that vocabulary is not so important in the quality of writing and is therefore not the writing teacher's job.) When I heard this question, I sighed and said, "If you believe that good vocabulary can make your students' papers more academic, accessible, and sophisticated, then yes, it is our job."

What the Research Says and Shows

Vocabulary most definitely plays a critical role in successful writing. First, insufficient vocabulary knowledge can limit students' ability to understand the sources they are reading. Second, simple vocabulary can make our ideas—and us—sound simple. Third, vocabulary errors make our writing sound awkward because we have either misused words or we have not used the words that NESs would use. Fourth, limited vocabulary can limit students' abilities to paraphrase or summarize academic material. Several decades of research have demonstrated that the level of vocabulary in our writing plays a significant role in the reader's overall perception of the quality of our writing. Recent research in corpus linguistics has helped writing teachers see how not knowing fixed expressions, collocations, transitions, and other formulaic language can prevent L2 students' writing from sounding advanced or academic.

Research to support the necessity of writing teachers to address vocabulary explicitly comes from two sources. First, research studies have examined which aspects of an essay are most likely to impact the way readers assess it. Second, various rubrics for scoring an essay numerically illustrate the extent to which vocabulary figures into the overall score of an essay.

Empirical Studies ——

The overall score that an essay receives can be impacted by a great number of factors, including content, grammar, mechanics, organization, spelling, and vocabulary. A substantial number of empirical studies have highlighted the effect that individual factors play in a paper's overall score. Figure 1.1 shows some of the studies that examine the role of vocabulary. Notice that not all of the findings are listed for each study; the focus is on the degree to which vocabulary knowledge contributes to the overall score of an essay. Notice also that "caveats" describe the limitations of some of the studies.

FIGURE 1.1. Empirical Studies of the Role of Vocabulary in ESL Essay Overall Scores

Research Study	Among the Findings
Hughes & Lascaratou (1982) 30 judges (10 native-speaker teachers of English, 10 Greek EFL teachers, 10 educated NESs) judged the seriousness of 32 errors made by Greek high school students.	*Caveat*: The 3 groups used different criteria for assessing the seriousness of errors. The Greek teachers made reference to the "basicness" of the errors. The native non-teachers used intelligibility as their main criterion. The native English teachers used both but leaned toward intelligibility.
Biber (1986) 545 real samples of spoken language (e.g., conversations, interviews, speeches, announcements) and written language (e.g., novels, editorial letters, press reports, academic prose) of approximately 2,000 words each were analyzed for differences in 41 key linguistic features.	1. Using different words (instead of repeating certain words) often results in using words with very specific meanings. (Conversely, using words with very specific meanings increases the number of different words used in a sample.) 2. Longer words convey more specialized meanings than shorter words. (Word length is a factor in vocabulary.)
Santos (1988) 178 professors at a U.S. university used a 10-point scale to assess two compositions written by NNSs.	1. Professors considered language more than content. 2. The most serious errors were lexical errors.

Ferris (1994) 28 text variables found in 160 university entrance placement exams (by 40 Arabic, 40 Chinese, 40 Japanese, 40 Spanish) were correlated with holistic scores assigned by three independent raters.	1. The top three variables that could predict holistic scores were all lexical in nature: number of words, synonymy/antonymy, and word length. 2. Higher proficiency students used a variety of lexical choices. 3. Students can benefit from encouragement in the areas of correct word choice, diversity in lexical/syntactic features, and use of cohesion and cohesive devices.
Engber (1995) 66 placement essays written by intermediate to advanced proficiency intensive English program students of different first languages were holistically scored. The overall holistic scores were analyzed for correlation with these four measures of lexical richness: lexical variation, error-free variation, percentage of lexical error, and lexical density.	1. High significant correlations were detected for (a) lexical variation, i.e., the ratio of different lexical items to the total number of lexical items in the essay (after adjusting for length) and (b) lexical variation minus error. 2. Of the four measures, the best correlation with overall holistic score was error-free lexical variation. Thus, a writer's ability to use many words and use them well was a strong predictor of a higher overall essay score.
Dordick (1996) 289 native-speaking college freshmen read one of ten versions of an ESL student's paragraph, with each version focusing on a specific error: poor rhetorical style (with no grammatical errors); article use; lexical errors; verb and subject-verb agreement; word order; prepositions; connectors and transitions; mixture of all errors; no errors (i.e., control).	Lexical errors (including inappropriate word choice or word form) and verb-related errors interfered with comprehension the most.
Pizarro (2003) 32 non-ESL trained raters were asked to (1) score holistically three university entrance compositions (representing low, middle, and high proficiency) and comment on the best and worst features of each, as well as (2) rate the severity of six error types in twelve example sentences (two sentences for each error type).	1. Grammar and vocabulary were noted as important as either best or worst aspects of the essays. (Limitation: this deals with only three specific essays not on the same topic.) 2. In the sentence errors, the three that were deemed most severe were grammar, organization, and vocabulary. *Caveats*: no statistical test for significance or effect size is reported; sentence error research is not as convincing as using real essays.

Rubrics for Scoring ESL Essays ——

In the previous section, we see that when raters are asked to evaluate essays in whatever manner they wish to do so, vocabulary is a good predictor of the overall score that an essay receives. In addition to this evidence from empirical research studies, we can also see the role assigned to vocabulary as reflected in actual rubrics used for scoring. Figure 1.2 shows that vocabulary counts for 25 percent of a typical university program rubric (Bryant, 1975), 20 percent of the widely used ESL Profile (Jacobs, Hartfield, Hughey, & Wormeth, 1981), and perhaps 15 percent of the TOEFL® scoring rubric. However, the empirical studies in Figure 1.1 hint that raters' perceptions of the vocabulary in an essay can also influence raters' perceptions of other categories and thereby pull up or pull down an essay's score. Thus, these figures of 25 percent, 20 percent, and 15 percent are at best the very <u>minimum</u> role of vocabulary in an essay's overall score. The bottom line: vocabulary clearly and significantly contributes to the overall score of an essay whether the essay is scored holistically or analytically.

FIGURE 1.2. Example Rubrics for Scoring ESL Writing Samples

Rubric	Criteria	Role of Vocabulary
Univ. of Missouri, Bryant (1975) (analytically scored on a 20-point system)	Four categories (20 points): 1. Treatment of subject and organization (5 points) 2. Vocabulary (5 points) 3. Errors (5 points) 4. Grammatical structures and complex sentences (5 points)	This scale is reflective of many program rubrics for evaluating ESL writing. Vocabulary counts 25 percent and is listed before grammar. In addition, "errors" could be any kind of error, including lexical.
ESL Profile © Jacobs et al. (1981) (analytically scored on a 100-point system; still widely used)	Five categories (100 points): 1. Content (30 points) 2. Organization (20 points) 3. Vocabulary (20 points) 4. Language Use (25 points) 5. Mechanics (5 points)	In this seminal instrument, vocabulary clearly counts 20 percent; however, vocabulary indirectly affects points in other areas because excelling in details, range, and support all depend on knowing more words. 1. Organization points can be gained for using "organizing vocabulary" such as *additionally, a second reason,* and *in conclusion.* 2. Content points are lost if a paper "lacks details" or has "limited range." 3. Organization points are lost in a paper with "limited support."

TOEFL® iBT 2004 (ETS) *Independent Writing Rubric* (holistically scored on a scale of 0–5, with 0 being low and 5 being high)	The four criteria used in awarding a score are: 1. how effectively the paper addresses the topic (content) 2. how well the paper is organized and developed 3. how well the paper displays unity, progression, and coherence 4. how well the paper displays consistent facility in language use	At least one of the subsets for each 0–5 score deals with language use, including vocabulary. In addition, we know that vocabulary is essential in assessing the other three criteria: content, organization/development, and unity/coherence. Specifically: 1. One of the four criteria for a score of 5 requires appropriate word choice and idiom usage. 2. One of the four criteria for a score of 4 requires a range of vocabulary but allows for errors in word form and idioms as long as they do not impede meaning. 3. Two of the four criteria for papers with a score of 3 mention vocabulary, specifically (a) inconsistent word choice and (b) limited vocabulary. 4. Two of the five criteria for a score of 2 note (a) inappropriate choice of words or word forms and (b) a large number of usage errors. 5. Papers scored 0 and 1 need basic language work.
TOEFL® iBT 2004 (ETS) *Integrated Writing Rubric* (holistically scored on a scale of 0–5, with 0 being low and 5 being high)	The main criteria revolve around a student's ability to comprehend material in a lecture and in a reading passage, select which parts from both are pertinent to a writing prompt, and then accurately combine the two. Thus, the two important overall areas are content and connection (e.g., organization, unity, accuracy).	All scores for this task depend on excellent comprehension of the listening passage and the reading passage, something that is impossible without good vocabulary knowledge. Similar to the *Independent Writing Rubric* (above), this rubric includes subsets for vocabulary and language use in each of its 0–5 scores. 1. Score 5: This requires response to the writing prompt with good organization and only occasional language errors. 2. Score 4: Papers have information that is vague or imprecise, with frequent or noticeable minor language errors. 3. Score 3: Papers are deficient in one of four categories, one of which includes frequent errors in grammar, usage, vague expressions, and/or obscured meanings. 4. Score 2: Paper is marked by significant language problems, omitted or wrong content, or incorrect connections between the lecture and the reading. 5. Scores 0–1: Papers need basic language work.

What We Can Do

1. **Teach vocabulary.**

   Now that we have seen that the vocabulary a writer uses in an essay influences the overall score given to the essay, not just the vocabulary score, it should be clear that students need to improve their active vocabulary in order to improve their writing. In other words, ESL writing teachers need to explicitly teach as much vocabulary as feasible—both early and often in our writing programs. Merely comprehending input or reading extensively will not suffice for the amount of vocabulary that a non-native speaker must learn to be able to compose well in English. Explicit instruction in specific vocabulary and in vocabulary learning strategies is essential.

2. **Teach the *right* vocabulary.**

   Your decision of which vocabulary to teach should be based entirely on an analysis of your learners' writing needs. *Why* are the students in a writing class? Are your students attempting to pass an exam such as the TOEFL® or another institutional barrier exam? Are they preparing to enroll in a college or university where they will soon have to take a general composition course? Are they graduate students who have to write a research report or even a thesis? What will they read in your class?

   Once you have focused on student vocabulary needs, your computer can be helpful. Two good sources of general academic English are the University Word List and the Academic Word List, both free and available on the Internet. (See Myth 3, Byrd and Bunting, for additional word list information.) The University Word List (Xue & Nation, 1984) consists of 808 vocabulary words that are common in academic texts. Academic materials were used as the data source because this list is designed to help NNSs who are in an academic setting—that is, those who want to study in high school, community college, or university. The Academic Word List (Coxhead, 2000) consists of

570 word families (e.g., *commit, commitment, committed, committing*) that occurred in more than half of the 28 academic subject areas. The academic corpus of 3,500,000 words from which the word families were pulled produced a list of academic words that are useful for the widest possible range of non-native learners of English. It is important for teachers to evaluate not only which words are included in these lists but how these lists were developed. It is easy to do a web search for current information on both these commonly used lists.

3. **Teach learners how to create their own lists of vocabulary that they need for writing.**
   Neither the University Word List nor the Academic Word List will suffice in meeting all your students' writing needs. The best strategy you can develop in your students is their ability to be aware of new vocabulary and to record new vocabulary items that they should then practice in their own writing.

   For example, if your students want to write a paper for a psychology class, they must learn to become aware of, or notice, the vocabulary that is used in psychology papers. Texts of this genre often contain vocabulary such as is *concerned with, mental processes,* and *schools of thought.* Likewise, if your students want to learn to write reports of an original science experiment that they have conducted, they might need words such as *purpose, intensity,* and *precise data.*

   Because our students have different academic goals in different fields, it should be clear that students must take the bulk of the responsibility to increase their vocabulary. Though explicit vocabulary instruction (from a book, a website, or a teacher) is an efficient way to learn vocabulary, the sheer volume of words to learn demands that the learner be aggressive in identifying new words to learn. Yes, teachers should teach vocabulary, but our students' writing cannot progress quickly enough with new vocabulary lessons from the teachers alone. One strategy students can use to learn vocabulary is to keep their own vocabulary list or notebook and to choose an organization method that increases the likelihood that they will actually open their notebooks *multiple times* to review vocabulary.

4. **Teach learners how to keep a vocabulary notebook that facilitates multiple retrievals of unknown or newly encountered vocabulary.**

Keeping a vocabulary list or notebook is one of the most effective and efficient techniques for students to assume the responsibility for learning vocabulary. However, it is imperative that students choose an organization method that increases the likelihood that they will actually open their notebooks *multiple times* to review vocabulary. (See Folse, 2006b, for an empirically based discussion on the necessity of multiple retrievals in learning L2 vocabulary.) In reality, if learners do not review what they have written in their vocabulary notebooks multiple times, then the notebook is useless, and student time should be spent on another task.

Vocabulary notebooks can be formatted in various ways. First, if students already have a system that works for them, they should definitely continue to follow that system. However, many ESL/EFL students believe that a vocabulary notebook is a mere list of English words on the left, with a translation on the right. Translations are good, but this type of list has limitations for multiple retrievals.

In *Vocabulary Myths* (Folse, 2004), I introduce a vocabulary notebook format with four pieces of information that allow four different ways to practice retrieval: with a synonym of the word, translation of the word from English to the L1, a translation of the L1 word to English, and a brief contextual example or collocation of the word. It is crucial that students lay out their vocabulary in a way that allows them to have those retrieval options. In addition, this notebook should be inviting (e.g., with lots of white space) so there is a greater chance that learners will revisit the page to retrieve meaning or form of the new words. Figure 1.3 shows an example of notebook entries for three vocabulary words written by a Spanish-speaking ESL student who is in a freshman psychology class. Notice how the student has skipped a line (or lines) between vocabulary entries and clearly lined up the information in two distinct columns.

FIGURE 1.3. A Learner's Vocabulary Notebook for Multiple Retrievals

1. enhance	aumentar, acrecentar
improve, make greater	"X" can _____ self-esteem.
2. hinder	dificular, impeder
delay, stop from happening	"Z" will _____ school success.
3. when it comes to "Y"	cuando se trata de "Y"
when you talk about "Y"	_____ literacy, I think . . .

With this design, each of the four pieces of information about each entry is in the same place on the page: The translation is always in the top right corner and the collocation always in the bottom right. Students can take a blank piece of paper, cut out one quarter of it, and slide the small open square up and down the notebook page, first with the open corner on the left and then on the right, to create four different practice questions. (See Folse, 2004, pp. 103–106, for a more thorough example and explanation of this technique.)

5. **Teach collocations, not just single words.**
   The traditional notion that a word is the letters between the space before and after it (e.g., *cat, out, bright*) is misguided at best. Vocabulary encompasses much more, including idioms (e.g., *let the cat out of the bag*), phrasal verbs (e.g., *run out of [money, time, energy]*), and collocations (e.g., *a bright future, dire circumstances*).

   While I believe that collocations are crucial to advanced writing, I want to make an especially strong case for the teaching of two specific categories of collocations: adjective + noun collocations *(different reason)* and adverb of degree + past participle as adjective + noun collocations *(widely known* or *widely known facts)*. First, collocations such as *bright future, negative impact,* and *empirical relationship* consist of a noun that is preceded by a specific adjective. In the case of *bright future,* we could substitute *good future* or *great future,* but neither pairing is as effective. In contrast, *bright future* sounds less like "basic ESL" and more like a combination that an NES might use in academic writing.

Second, collocations such as *internationally distributed, widely criticized,* and *significantly reduced rates* consist of an adverb of degree followed by a past participle used as an adjective, which may be a predicate adjective or an adjective preceding a noun. Compare these sentences:

<u>Basic</u>: These products are distributed in many countries.

<u>Better</u>: These products are internationally distributed.

<u>Basic</u>: More people in Argentina read *El Clarin* than any other newspaper.

<u>Better</u>: The most widely read newspaper in Argentina is *El Clarin.*

Helping students identify these collocations and learn them involves an acceptance by teachers that there is a strong link between academic reading and academic writing. In a two-step process, teachers should first train students to recognize or be sensitive to collocations in their academic reading material by, for example, asking students to underline whole phrases (as opposed to words only) that they may not know or may not understand well. Second, teachers should identify and explain the most useful and most frequently used collocations with the entire class. If students are keeping a vocabulary notebook, they should add these collocations to their list.

6. **Test vocabulary. Hold learners accountable.**

It is a well-known principle in education that learners tend to learn what is expected of them and usually—and unfortunately for teachers—not much more, so we must persuade students of the importance of vocabulary and then repeatedly hold them accountable for their vocabulary learning in quizzes and exams.

7. **Teach paraphrasing and summarizing.**
In courses ranging from remedial to graduate work, many academic writing assignments require students to read one or more original sources and then synthesize them into one original piece of writing. This process of synthesis is quite complex, involving sophisticated reading strategies and writing skills such as paraphrasing and summarizing.

In reading, vocabulary is essential: Not knowing even a handful of words can prevent comprehension. Next, students must paraphrase the key ideas, at least partially with another set of word and phrase synonyms to avoid plagiarism. Then students must be able to reduce the key paraphrased ideas to the most important points and then be able to weave the points from various sources—that is, to synthesize the ideas. While summarizing and synthesizing tend to have their own set of key vocabulary items (e.g., *on one hand, in conclusion, both*), reading comprehension and paraphrasing will require knowledge of an extremely large number of vocabulary items, including not only single words but also idioms, phrasal verbs, and collocations.

8. **Make sure that explicit teaching of vocabulary is included in the writing program from the lowest levels of language proficiency.**
Learning vocabulary in a second language is a daunting task because of the sheer quantity of single words, phrases, idioms, collocations, and other lexical chunks. (For further discussion about lexical bundles, see Myth 2, Schuemann, and Myth 6, Conrad, in this volume.) In addition, learners must understand multiple aspects for each: its form and spelling, its pronunciation, its meaning(s), its connotations, its most common usages, and its register(s). All these aspects are even more complicated for L2 academic writing, so advanced ESL/EFL writers need sub-

stantial repertoires of words, especially synonyms, nuanced connotations, and collocations—a huge task. The necessary time for the accumulation of such a vocabulary indicates that the study of basic academic vocabulary should begin early in the L2 learning process, not only in reading classes but in every ESL/EFL class.

Further, research studies presented in this chapter have shown that readers value the writer's words in their evaluation of the writer's message. Commonly used assessment rubrics give substantial weight to vocabulary—either directly or indirectly. That is, vocabulary errors can play a more important role in influencing readers than grammatical errors, yet ESL writing curricula continue to be dominated by grammar discussions. Instead, or at least in addition, writing programs must address vocabulary.

In conclusion, learning each new word in a second language is never a simple yes-no proposition. Neither teachers nor students should equate knowing a word with a light switch that has only two options: on and off. Instead, we should think of a dimmer switch that can be cranked up (or down) in varying increments. Is vocabulary explicitly covered in our teaching materials? Is vocabulary systematically covered in our courses? Do our writing rubrics address vocabulary? Are students in our writing classes keeping a vocabulary notebook that they use for multiple retrievals? Only when we can answer "yes" to these questions will we demonstrate a true commitment to teaching vocabulary in our ESL/EFL writing courses.

Further Reading

In *Vocabulary Myths* (2004), I describe more fully the numerous reasons to teach vocabulary in all ESL classes.

For a useful synopsis, read Appendix A: Ten Things You Should Know about Teaching ESL/EFL Vocabulary in *The Art of Teaching Speaking: Research and Pedagogy for the ESL/EFL Classroom* (Folse, 2006a, pp. 228–234).

Questions for Reflection

1. To what extent do you think that vocabulary in a given piece of writing impacts a reader's perception of the quality of that piece of writing?

2. What do you think ESL writers believe about the role of vocabulary knowledge in the quality of their writing. Interview three ESL students to hear their opinions about vocabulary and their writing.

3. In composition classes that you have taught (or observed), how extensively and systematically is vocabulary knowledge addressed?

4. How important is vocabulary in paraphrasing? Find a quote of three to five sentences from an expert on a current topic (e.g., a scientist or politician). Write a concise paraphrase of the original. Now notice which synonyms you used for which original words. (Also, note which original words you did not include in the paraphrase. Remember that in order to know not to include them [because they are not important enough] you have to actually know those words, too.)

5. For further study and discussion, ask three native speakers and three non-native speakers to perform the task in Number 4. Compare the paraphrases in terms of vocabulary. Which group uses a better variety of synonyms?

6. Look at the curriculum for an upper-intermediate or advanced ESL writing class. Identify specific teaching objectives for: (a) composition (i.e., writing, editing, brainstorming, etc.), (b) grammar, and (c) vocabulary. What do your results show about the myth discussed in this chapter?

7. Good examples of composed, crafted writing can often be found in editorial columns in large newspapers or magazines. Choose a selection from one of these columns to analyze. Can you identify collocations that make the writing sound appropriate for this venue?

    Are these collocations likely to be known by an NNS? Be sure to differentiate "known" in the passive sense (i.e., students can understand the collocation when they read it) from the active sense (i.e., students are able to retrieve this collocation from their English vocabulary knowledge and use it on their own).

8. Several teaching suggestions were made at the end of the chapter to help students improve the vocabulary used in their writing. Can you think of other concrete suggestions?

References

Biber, D. (1986). Spoken and written textual dimensions in English: Resolving the contradictory findings. *Language, 62*(2), 384–414.

Bryant, W. (1975). On grading compositions objectively. *The Canadian Modern Language Review/La Revue Canadienne des Langues Vivantes, 31* (3), 260–263.

Coxhead, A. (2000). A new academic word list. *TESOL Quarterly, 34*(2), 213–238.

Dordick, M. (1996). Testing for a hierarchy of the communicative interference of errors. *System, 24*(3), 299–308.

Educational Testing Services. (2004). *Scoring guides (rubics) for writing responses.* Princeton, NJ: ETS.

Engber, C. (1995). The relationship of lexical proficiency to the quality of ESL compositions. *Journal of Second Language Writing, 4*(2), 139–155.

Ferris, D. (1994). Lexical and syntactic features of ESL writing by students at different levels of L2 proficiency. *TESOL Quarterly, 28*(2), 414–420.

Folse, K. (2004). *Vocabulary myths: Applying second language research to classroom teaching.* Ann Arbor: University of Michigan Press.

———. (2006a). *The art of teaching speaking: Research and pedagogy for the ESL/EFL classroom.* Ann Arbor: University of Michigan Press.

———. (2006b). The effect of type of written exercise on L2 vocabulary retention. *TESOL Quarterly, 40*(2), 273–293.

Hughes, A., & Lascaratou, C. (1982). Competing criteria for error gravity. *ELT Journal, 36*(3), 175–182.

Jacobs, H., Hartfiel, V., Hughey, J., & Wormuth, D. (1981). *Testing ESL composition: A practical approach.* Boston: Newbury House.

Pizarro, M. (2003). A study of different composition elements that raters respond to. *Estudios Ingleses de la Universidad Complutense, 11*, 53–72.

Santos, T. (1988). Professors' reactions to the academic writing of non-native-speaking students. *TESOL Quarterly, 22*(1), 69–90.

Xue, G. & Nation, I.S.P. (1984). A university word list. *Language Learning and Communication, 3*(2), 215–229.

Teaching Citation Is Someone Else's Job

Cynthia M. Schuemann
Miami Dade College

In the Real World

I SHARE AN OFFICE WITH A FACULTY MEMBER from the psychology department. As I opened our door yesterday, I encountered a slew of term papers from her students who had shoved wistful rewrites under the door in hopes of improving their final grades. The most glaring comment on the attached originals was, "Fix copy and paste!" I soon learned that Professor Abety's "copy-and-paste" comment was her label for plagiarism. Such copy-and-paste of research material is a pervasive practice, especially for ESL writers.

The urban community college where I teach, Miami Dade (MDC), has seven different campuses with large EAP departments. The topic of responsibility for addressing citation was first debated by ESL writing faculty at MDC in 2000 when a cross-campus team was in the process of developing course competencies to meet new state guidelines. Our program's original writing competencies had been created in the 1980s, and they included no mention of citation. Due to ongoing resistance, the current competencies still only include one limited reference to citation, at the last level of writing instruction: "The student will appropriately credit sources in a basic manner."

As with most institutions, any programmatic change happens slowly. There is comfort in continuing with "what we have been doing for years," but in contrast with some of my traditionalist colleagues, I think ESL students are done a disservice if attention to citation and appropriate alternatives to copy-and-paste "writing" are not addressed in program-wide systematic ways in ESL writing classes. Students need to feel comfortable with this crucial aspect of writing prior to exiting an ESL program. Yet even in 2007, with ongoing state-wide discussion and drafting of a new set of EAP learning outcomes, our cross-campus teams continue to debate the value of a significant citation strand in our curriculum. It is taking persistence to gain consensus on the importance of including citation in ESL objectives. Further, even though writing competencies or learning outcomes theoretically guide instructional practices across the college, what actually happens once the classroom doors are closed depends mostly on the beliefs and practices of individual instructors.

One of the main reasons for resistance to teaching citation is that many ESL writing faculty members see our primary goal as preparing students for freshman composition. In contrast, I argue that first-year composition tasks are only one small slice of the writing expectations students quickly encounter. College students take many general education courses, and they need to hand in written work and give presentations in discipline-specific classes early on. In order for them to feel confident about these assignments, we need to teach ESL students appropriate and effective ways to include and credit the ideas of others in their writing and provide our students with ample opportunities to practice.

As Keith Folse mentions in Myth 1 in this volume, he found himself feeling angry when his students turned in papers with plagiarized phrases, and my officemate, Professor Abety, has frequently asked, "Do they think we're stupid?!" while grading papers. Keith noted that after conferencing with one of his students, he realized that students need to know more than that plagiarism is wrong; we must help them find their own voices, especially in a micro-sense—their own words and expressions, even when they believe that the original author "says it better." With the Internet offering such easy access to "copy-and-paste" material, we must take responsibility for teaching citation throughout our ESL writing programs.

What the Research Says and Shows

Working with the words and ideas of others is a crucial part of all learning experiences. Ironically, research about citation can most easily be explored by reading studies that investigate plagiarism, or cases of failure to cite in ways expected by college and university faculty in English-speaking countries. Plagiarism is a topic that crosses disciplines and touches emotions because integrity, values, and ethics are part of the discussion. Three of the most common disciplines reporting research on academic dishonesty, including plagiarism, are library and information science, education, and psychology (Ercegovac & Richardson, 2004). These disciplines are an indication of the breadth of inquiry in this area and an illustration of how the issue is not isolated to ESL settings.

In terms of research that explores relationships between second language learning and citing the ideas or direct quotations of others, three important studies provide essential and recent findings on the issue. First, Pennycook (1996) establishes the need to consider plagiarism from a cross-cultural perspective. Second, Shi (2006) provides a window on learner concerns regarding citation. And third, Abasi, Akbari, & Graves (2006) study the progress of language learners in developing writing practices that include effective source references as they come to feel stronger identity associations within discipline areas. The findings from these three studies can provide an understanding of the complexity of the issue as well as a rationale for including writing assignments with citation expectations as part of ESL curricula. Figure 2.1 summarizes the pertinent results of these three studies.

FIGURE 2.1. Research on Writing with the Words of Others

Observation	Study	Among the Findings
We need to better understand relationships between text, memory, learning and culture.	Pennycook (1996) An extensive literature review and interviews with Chinese university students.	1. "Ownership" of text is a geographic (cultural) and historical construct. 2. Awareness of diverse cultural/educational practices with respect to using the words of others can enhance understanding of different behaviors and attitudes with respect to plagiarism. 3. In academic settings, many current plagiarism response practices are "pedagogically unsound and intellectually arrogant" (p. 226).
Novice writers are uncertain about which words they need to cite and acknowledge in their writing.	Shi (2006) At a Canadian university, 46 undergraduate students from five different language backgrounds were interviewed on issues of textual appropriation.	1. College students interpret the concept of plagiarism in diverse ways related to L1 backgrounds and prior educational experiences. 2. L2 writers of English often view imitation of language as part of the learning process and not as appropriation of text. 3. Current advances in technology, accessibility of electronic text, and practices in collaborative writing and research contribute to L2 writers' challenges with respect to acknowledgement conventions.
We need to increase student awareness of the relationship between writing and identity.	Abasi, Akbari, & Graves (2006) A qualitative study investigating the writings of five graduate students at a Canadian university during the course of a semester.	Inappropriate borrowing is related to a student's level of "enculturation" into discipline discourses. 1. Increasing levels of enculturation lead to increased awareness of identity options in social contexts. 2. The roots of "plagiarism" by ESL students lie in their limited "knowing" and their view of text as authoritative.

Citation and its negative correlate, plagiarism, are cultural and complex topics. First, a clear sense of definition of these two terms can serve to anchor the summaries of the three studies that support early integration of practice with citation in expository writing for ESL students. *The American Heritage Dictionary* (2007) defines *citation* as the act of paraphrasing or the direct quotation of "an authoritative source for substantiation" of an essay writer's ideas, and *Wikipedia*[1] (2007) clarifies: that plagiarism is

> the unauthorized use or close imitation of the language and thoughts of another author and the representation of them as one's own original work. Unlike cases of forgery, in which the authenticity of the writing, document, or some other kind of object, itself is in question, plagiarism is concerned with the issue of false attribution.

Citation, then, is more than appropriately crediting sources in "a basic manner." It includes selecting and locating an authoritative source whose words and ideas can support a student writer's belief or cultural experience regarding an academic topic. Further, plagiarism is a concept of great complexity with deep levels of interpretation and consequence. I believe that all educators should develop a clear personal understanding of plagiarism that is relevant to their student populations and academic settings. The three studies summarized in Figure 2.1 offer critical perspectives on plagiarism and citation.

First, Alastair Pennycook (1996), from the University of Melbourne in Australia, published a much referenced study on plagiarism, and he has continued research in this area. He explained that the idea that text is an author's property and use of it without proper citation is a "crime" is a Western perspective. And, while legal protections (such as copyright laws) against the "theft" of words or ideas find historical basis in Western traditions, Pennycook questions that moralistic stance.

When teaching English in China, Pennycook first came to realize that for Chinese students, handing in writing assignments they had memorized from the writings of authorities as writing assignments was considered acceptable. Further, he found that memorization of text as a

---

[1] Even though *Wikipedia* may be considered a controversial reference source by some, I consulted several dictionaries seeking an effective definition of **plagiarism** for the purposes of this selection. The elements included in the *Wikipedia* definition here were, I felt, most helpful in making the concept more transparent.

way of learning is more valued in Chinese culture than in Western societies, which tend to place greater value on individualism and "original" thinking. Pennycook also describes receiving a student essay about Abraham Lincoln that was correctly written, but seemed odd. Another student revealed that the words used were from a high school textbook passage that had been memorized. The first student indicated that he had felt lucky to be asked to write on a topic that he already knew something about. This incident led Pennycook to research culturally different perspectives on text ownership.

Pennycook's illustration and subsequent student-interview research findings have been useful for me in two ways: first, to remind me that my perspective of "cut and paste" copying reflects my own cultural bias, and second, to reconsider how remembering information as it is written (memorizing) contributes to learning.

Regarding cultural bias, Pennycook argues that many current plagiarism response practices are "pedagogically unsound and intellectually arrogant" (p. 226). Although a strong characterization, I agree that much baggage is associated with issues of plagiarism; as a result, educators' responses to instances of copying range from oblivious ignorance to student expulsion. That diversity of response is not helpful to students. Further, many factors may contribute to "academic dishonesty" on the part of students: response to stressful workloads, resistance to assignments seen lacking in personal value, insecurity or fear of failure, increasing use of collaborative learning practices, uncertainty about norms and consequences, and even increasing societal evidence of plagiarism—including professional writers and recent newspaper article writers.

In short, I think teachers err if they take an act of student copying as a personal insult and respond emotionally. Further, an instructor who expresses suspicion with a judgmental tone may evoke an immediately defensive response from the student. Clearly, if a student does not sense having done something wrong, no resolution can be reached. Instead, we teachers can benefit from developing initial non-judgmental responses to student copying and committing to our responsibility to make students aware of the meaning of plagiarism, while being aware of culturally diverse norms associated with copying. On the other hand, students can and should learn the norms of academic research writing, including citation conventions in academic writing, throughout their writing processes.

Regarding memorizing and writing, Pennycook's work has led me to see a further contradiction in Western academic practice. We do expect written, even rote, retelling of some concept explanations in short answer/essay exams, often in the exact words of others, and often without citation. Between instructor and student there is an assumed understanding of the textbook/lecture source. This may be an additional point of confusion for students in understanding when "copying" is appropriate and when it is not. Moreover, it challenges a myth that writing the words of others is essentially rote learning. Retelling can deepen understanding and knowing. When is it acceptable for students in English-speaking countries to use the words of others, such as imitating to demonstrate knowledge, without citation, and when is it unacceptable?

Ling Shi, from the University of British Columbia in Vancouver, Canada, has also investigated relationships between student cultural backgrounds and text appropriation beliefs and practices in English. Shi (2006) conducted interview research with 46 undergraduate students from five different language backgrounds: English (n=11), German (n=10), Japanese (n=9), Chinese (n=8), and Korean (n=8). Her work confirms Pennycook's findings that student writers from non-English speaking backgrounds perceive plagiarism differently from faculty in English-medium institutions. For example, in Shi's study, 12 of the 25 Asian participants had never even heard of plagiarism prior to coming to North America; "word ownership" was literally a foreign concept. Further, when asked to translate the word *plagiarism* into Japanese, Chinese, and Korean, students' responses were revealing: The idea did not have immediate and transparent equivalents in the other languages.

Shi also found that the majority of NNS (24 of 35 non-native speakers) believed that paraphrasing and summarizing the ideas of others was a language-learning challenge. They indicated a struggle with lack of vocabulary and noted that they had learned much of their English through imitation. Although most recognized that an action such as buying a complete paper online and claiming authorship would be wrong, it was less clear how using "pieces" of writing was wrong. How can students "put something in their own words" when English is not their own language? Does substituting synonyms count? Thus, Shi's findings confirm the complexity of plagiarism and affirm the need to provide ESL writing students with opportunities to develop skill in citation.

The synonym question came up recently in one of my writing classes when a student found such joy in learning the right-click synonym trick in Microsoft Word. Working with synonyms to paraphrase is a good start, but it can also lead to some awkward collocations as well as questions about appropriate-use boundaries. For example, a student recently wrote, *Some people live in poor neighborhoods where they see a lot of violence and <u>necessity</u>; <u>subsequently</u> they are <u>influenced</u> by stress. Discrimination is another source in which stress <u>takes place</u>*. A cross-check with Word's thesaurus leads me to these synonyms offered for the underlined words: *need, consequently, affect,* and *occur.* It is evident that this student has used some copy and paste, and she is struggling to find ways to express ideas she wants to communicate in an academic voice. Replacing the synonyms in the first sentence results in something that was closer to the original and sounds less awkward: *Some people live in poor neighborhoods where they see a lot of violence and <u>need</u>; <u>consequently</u> they are <u>affected</u> by stress.*

Finally, two-thirds (31 of 46) of Shi's participants were concerned with avoiding plagiarism as novice writers, including 7 of 11 of the NESs. That is, a majority of both groups, native and non-native speakers of English, felt insecure when making writing decisions concerning sources. For example, some participants doubted that ideas belonged to people, and they felt that many people could have the same idea, including the students themselves. In other words, if a student agreed with an idea or opinion, then it was also his/hers on some level (Shi, 2006). Another area of uncertainty was whether or not collaborating, discussing, and sharing ideas with other students that later became part of writing was different from copying. Further, students were unclear about how many words could be copied or "imitated" without being considered plagiarism. In addition, they wondered how to distinguish general knowledge that may not need citation from specific knowledge that would, and they wondered about having to cite when an author got the information from another author. All of these issues are worthy to discuss in ESL writing classes, and clearly student writers want to learn how to write confidently with sources.

Students in Shi's study (2006) felt uncertain about what and how many words they might copy without reprisal, and they recognized that the original text of a NES (native English speaker) authority was more effective than their "own words." The disparities between faculty and ESL student perceptions of plagiarism is a challenge for both students and teachers. ESL students must therefore have ample opportunities in the "safe" environment of their writing classes to explore new expressions, test out synonyms, and learn about boundaries of idea and word ownership.

The final study (Abasi, Akbari, & Graves, 2006) considers relationships between identity and writing. This qualitative study investigated the writings of five NNS graduate students at a Canadian university during the course of a semester. At the master's level, enculturation into a discipline is profound, and heightened exposure to course assignment readings such as journal articles more regularly allows students to experience discipline-specific writing styles. The authors determined that increasing levels of enculturation led to increased awareness of identity options in social contexts—plagiarism diminishes when students become more enculturated in disciplinary discourses. In contrast, the researchers found that misappropriation of text occurred more frequently among the first-year NNS graduate students. That is, they observed that the root of plagiarism for these newer students was in their limited "knowing" and their view of text as authoritative. However, as these students increased their interactions with source material, they also developed their command of discipline-specific ideas and expressions, increased their use of acceptable vocabulary/synonyms, and used more appropriate writing strategies.

These findings correspond with the research results of Pennycook and Shi: ESL students can develop understanding of U.S. academic citation conventions, and they can put their knowledge into practice. These are, I think, hopeful results.

In contrast to the graduate students in Shi's research, Abasi, Akbari, & Graves (2006) noted that undergraduates are required to take coursework comprising diverse general education fields, with two or three sets of citation formats and conventions among them. Moreover, the citation and plagiarism information they receive from their general education course instructors is limited at best and almost certainly confusing. It is little wonder that undergraduates struggle with the concepts and accurate use of citation conventions.

If the uses and selection of citation seem complex, they are—far too complicated to simply "add on" to a final-course, final-assignment research paper. Because our ESL writing students (and many of Shi's NES writers as well) consider themselves "novice" U.S. academic writers, the challenge to learn citation conventions—and meet and beat the plagiarism challenge as well—will take teacher explanation and expertise and student patience and practice, practice, practice. To effectively meet these challenges, work must begin early in an ESL writing program and focus on instruction with citation and avoidance of plagiarism as a major goal of the program. ESL writing classes are simply the best place for students to experiment with finding the balance between learning how to credit the words and ideas of others in accordance with English conventions, while learning new ways to express themselves in English at the same time.

What We Can Do

If an ESL writing program incorporates time and practice opportunities to citation conventions as it does with other important rhetorical conventions, spiraling the tasks from introductory to more sophisticated levels of knowledge as students progress through the program, students should feel relatively comfortable and confident as they enter their undergraduate general education courses. For example, if students begin to read introductory authoritative sources about general education topics (from psychology, science, and history textbooks, for example) and begin to learn summary skills; if they then move to sources that include in-text and end-of-text citations and practice paraphrase skills; and if they then move to constructing paragraphs and essays that contain authoritative materials, their research strategies will improve as their academic writing strategies improve. And if, during that same time, teachers offer students clear definitions and examples of plagiarism, and ongoing exercises to avoid plagiarizing, students will better understand the conventions they are practicing.

Eleven specific suggestions for teachers and students, as well as exercises that can cross a variety of language proficiency levels, follow.

1. **Teachers must acknowledge (as this chapter has shown) the challenges L2 speakers face when responding to source material or integrating it into their writing.**

   For undergraduates in particular, these challenges include their (a) limited lexicons, (b) limited levels of enculturation in college discourse communities, and (c) culturally different perspectives on text authority and reference conventions. When teachers convey acknowledgment and understanding of these challenges rather than being judgmental, students become more open to learning. Then we need to regularly include discussion of these three challenges ESL student writers face.

   Second, teachers need to guide students to discovering more about what lies ahead in their academic journeys at college and foster connections. (Suggested sources for some of this information can be found in Suggestions 3 and 4.) For example, we need to plan lecture and discussion activities to inform students about different perspectives on text authority and citation conventions. It is important to explore with students the perhaps surprising U.S. academic culture's belief that words are owned, and that copying them as if a student owned them is perceived as stealing. Some interesting public case examples of plagiarism, even one involving Helen Keller, can be found on the *Wikipedia* site under the topic of plagiarism. (Another related activity is described in Suggestion 10.)

2. **Preview potential vocabulary and effective expressions with students before they write.**

   Students believe that they need more words and that learning vocabulary is important, so teachers need to support students in taking concrete actions to expand their word repertoires in writing. (A vocabulary activity suggestion is included below in item three.) As both Folse and Conrad discuss in this volume, ongoing consciousness-raising about vocabulary, including lexical bundles, is crucial for ESL writers. Even more important than content vocabulary in writing classes is teaching conventional "glue words"—an expressive label for function words that resonates with students. For example, as part of brainstorming before writing (in addition to making concept maps or outlines), I also have the students anticipate words or expressions they might want to include in their writing by using a three-column list. Figure 2.2 is an example "word brainstorm" that I provide for low intermediate–level student writers about a science topic.

FIGURE 2.2. Word Brainstorming

Content Words	Glue Words	Reporting Words
biomed	refers to	state(s)
species	means	note(s)
habitat	there are	indicate(s)
niche	includes	mention(s)
community	consists of	
ecosystem	in other words	
environment	for example	
	first, second, third	
	one _____ , another	
	characteristic	
	aspect	

Just as previewing vocabulary is valuable for ESL students before reading and listening, it is equally valuable before writing to provide students with expressive tools that work at least as well as copied phrases. Lists can be derived from (and expanded upon) any relevant text appropriate to the proficiency level. For instance, before writing a summary, students can read and highlight a reading selection for content and glue words to list.

3. **Teach students about the concept of idiolect.**

Idiolect refers to each individual's unique way of expressing himself or herself. To help students grasp this concept, I compare idiolect to a thumbprint. No two people say things in exactly the same way, even if they are talking about something similar. For example, you might ask the students in your class to take out a sheet of paper and write a definition for the word *identity* or any other relevant concept word. Collect the papers, and read a selection of the definitions out loud. List the words and phrases that occur frequently on the board; note that no two are identical (though there are common words and phrases), and not one would be identical to a definition found in a dictionary. Throughout the semester, as students work with the words of others, mentioning idiolect again helps them to better sense the difference between imitating to acquire new English vocabulary/expressions and copying. "Idiolect?" written beside a suspect student sentence or phrase is a word that can convey a concise positive reminder message to "use your own words" rather than the more accusatory "copy and paste." Another practical example of making an idiolect connection in skills classes is when my students write a definition for the term *psychology* on one of their reading tests. Many of the students will start, *Psychology is the science that seeks to understand. . . .* As I read a set of their definitions out loud to the class, it becomes clear that this is someone else's idiolect, and the students quickly learn that they need to add, at least, *According to our textbook. . . .*

4. **Take a top-down approach to curricular planning.**

The more we know about our institutional academic communities, even informally, the easier it is to plan a relevant, authentic writing program. For instance, most colleges and universities can provide ready information about enrollment patterns. On a regular basis, I visit a link on one of our college websites called the Top 100 Courses. For example, for the last fall semester, in terms of general education courses (excluding English and math), I can see at a glance that the most seats were taken in introductory courses in computer usage, psychology, humanities, biology, economics, critical thinking/ethics, philosophy, human anatomy, nutrition, social environment, music appreciation, energy/natural environment, art appreciation, sociology, jazz and pop music, financial accounting, literature, business, education, and chemistry. Because this list is ordered by frequency of enrollment, I can see that a computer-based writing course with some work based on psychology would be potentially helpful for many of my community college students. Further, sharing this information will allow my students to become more aware of the general education courses required for their majors, and they can prepare for those courses with authentic coursework, even at lower language levels of proficiency in the ESL writing program.

The second top-down factor I consider prior to the first class meeting is declared majors that are listed on my class roll. For instance, for the next term I see architecture, biology, business administration, computer science, criminal justice, medical technician, nursing, pharmacy, and pre–bachelor of arts. Even though this list represents great diversity, knowing students' potential majors helps me plan more relevant writing assignments to better meet student needs. I can show students actual writing assignments from their selected major fields (or fields of interest) and develop assignments appropriate to their language proficiency that will also help them prepare for future. For the students, working on writing in common discipline discourses is motivating, and it can influence their future course selections as well as provide a foundation for disciplinary acculturation.

A spiraled approach across a writing curriculum that integrates writing activities related to some of the high-frequency general core courses works best. Students can practice integrating elements of retelling, paraphrase, quotation, summary, interpretation, elaboration, and reflection in their writing. Low-intermediate writers can locate popular websites about topics of interest, learn to take notes about the topic, orally present "interesting facts" to their classmates about those topics (formally or informally), and begin to learn summary skills. More advanced student writers can add such activities as using database searches for additional information, integrating in-text and end-of-text citations, and balancing secondary materials with their own reflections and interpretations. As students increase their confidence in the knowledge of some the boundaries of word/expression/idea ownership, attention can turn to some of the conventions and expectations of working with the words of others in more particular disciplines in advanced ESL writing classes.

5. **Expose students to many examples of citations in readings and in student writing.**
   It is important for the students to see both in-text and end-of-text citations in authentic use to enhance their awareness of applied practice. Often students read textbook materials without noticing how authors use citation. In approaches similar to raising awareness of "hooks" in introductions, the use of transition words reflecting rhetorical modes, and other elements of paragraph/essay structure, so should attention be called to effective reference use. Even students with limited language proficiency can highlight examples of citation in academic texts (as shown on p. 33). Psychology textbooks are good sources for citation examples due to the experimental nature of research in

this discipline area. To illustrate, this excerpt comes from a freshman-level textbook at my college:

> There is no shortage of reading material regarding the value of meditative practice (Goleman, 1977; Kabat-Zinn, 1990; Ram Dass, 1990). Nor is there any lack of scientific research demonstrating that the practice of meditation indeed works to reduce and relieve pain (Kabat-Zinn, 1990), to lower blood pressure and the advance of atherosclerosis (Benson, 1984; Ornish, 1992) and to facilitate general healing. (Abascal, Bruak, Stephenson, Bricato, 2006, 199)

The first step is for students to see the names. The second step is to read the preceding sentence and then to associate a researcher with a study, theory, or concept. The teacher or student pairs could create a matching exercise; then students might match the in-text citation with end-of-text citations found in the text's bibliography. Finally, the teacher can point out that a text example such as this includes a greater density of citation than a student paper would, and follow the activity by repeating the same exercise with a student research paper model. (Faculty who require research papers in freshman-level courses at the college may be willing to share exemplary student papers.)

6. **Use the reference librarian and library materials as resources.** To expose students to discipline-specific writing samples, library connections are essential. First, librarians keep up with resources that are evolving with lightening speed, and their job is to share that information. While some ESL teachers may resist teaching citation because they feel out of touch, librarians can help. They might come to a class to do a presentation on using databases or work with citation formats such as APA or MLA. They offer library tours and develop "scavenger hunt" exercises for students. Helping students to establish early ongoing rela-

tionships with institutional librarians can benefit them—and their teachers.

For instance, college students today often encounter journal articles in electronic formats housed in databases, but libraries also still maintain some hard-copy collections. Not long ago, I realized that my students did not actually know what an academic journal was. When I asked what a journal was, the first response was that it was a kind of diary, and then one student asked, "a newspaper?" So, exploring the journals section in the library can result in new knowledge about discipline writing and a chance to contrast popular journals with academic journals. The library also has introductory textbooks from different discipline areas that students (or teachers) can preview and use for writing assignment source material.

7. **If you have access to tools such as *Turnitin.com*, use them in formative ways.**
   Turnitin.com is a software system that detects use of text from Internet sources. If your institution subscribes to this or another anti-plagiarism service, take advantage. With Turnitin, teachers store student-written work in class sections. The program gives a percentage score based on how much of the work is "copy and paste" from an Internet source. The software highlights exact lines and phrases in each student text and lists the original author. This is quite eye-opening for ESL students. It addresses some of their unease about how much of a phrase they can imitate without having it be considered plagiarism, and they feel less threatened because they can get this feedback on a draft, without reprisal, without any personal contact. Then they are able to make changes either by appropriately crediting a source, or by modifying how they express themselves prior to having a paper read by a teacher. Using a program like Turnitin is also a relief for teachers. There are times when teachers read something and know it does not represent a student's idiolect, but it

is hard to deal with a student who might insist that the work is original. Turnitin can provide an objective perspective.

8. **Lead students to the wealth of internet support tools for citation use.**

www.dianahacker.com/resdoc/

This site has excellent support for students writing with sources, and it is user friendly to navigate. On the opening page students can select from support for writing in four discipline areas: humanities, social sciences, history, and science. There is help on finding sources, documenting sources, and sample student papers.

www.citationmachine.net

This site helps students to write correct end-of-text and in-text citations in APA, MLA, or Chicago styles. Students fill in boxes with information as specified, such as last name, first initial with a period, book title with only the first word capitalized, etc. Then they submit and get a version of the citation they can copy and paste into a Word document.

Some databases (many of those on EBSCO, for example) now provide students with a citation for each article the student locates, which students can copy and paste (without fear of reprisal) into their end-of-text citation list. However, students must understand that neither this nor any other citation program is perfect (not even those on databases like EBSCO). That means students who use such programs must understand what problems exist and what they need to add, subtract, and/or change before each citation will be complete and correct. Still, the advantage of having a partially correct citation is that students need only to learn the three to five changes necessary rather than the two to three dozen decisions that are part of every citation.

www.lib.umn.edu/help/calculator/

This site helps students calculate an assignment timeline for writing research papers. Students fill in a box with the due date and discipline area, and the assignment calculator provides a list of twelve steps to be completed with due dates. Steps include understanding the assignment and selecting and focusing the topic, etc., as well as collecting, evaluating, and working with source material. Each step has links with help if students are unclear about how to carry out a step.

9. **Help students develop autonomy.**

Provide students with hands-on practice in various ways to interpret the writings of others while giving credit to original authors. Help students to see the importance and value of including the voices of others in their own writing while avoiding plagiarism or misuse of text. Some basic practice activities that help students learn how to do this in English follow:

- Develop sentence structure scaffolding charts for your students, and keep them accessible, for example, posted on a wall if possible. Figure 2.3 gives students information about how to work with the phrase *According to . . .* and definitions.

FIGURE 2.3. Scaffolding Chart: According to . . .

According to	Last Name or Source Name	(year)	concept	glue words for defining: *mean(s), is/are, refer(s) to*	explanation

- Teach students the most common reporting verbs and their frequent use patterns. Although used in conversation more than writing, *says* is a useful verb to practice regularly in class. When students make statements, the quick question, "Who says?" helps them learn to qualify with a last name or simple reference to "our textbook." In reality, last names are not easy for ESL students to develop fluency with. For example, the names found in the psychology excerpt in Suggestion 4 are Goleman,

Kabat-Zinn; Ram Dass, Benson, and Ornish. "Who says?" *Ornish says* reinforces the common pattern.

Using the Vocabulary Profile on the Complete Lexical Tutor (Cobb, n.d.), I found that some of the highest frequency reporting verbs in English include *say, state, note, point out, mention, claim, describe, explain,* and *compare.* Reporting verbs I found on the Academic Word List (AWL) (Coxhead, 2000) include *indicate, maintain, emphasize, stress,* and *deny.* (For a description of the AWL, see Myth 1, Folse, and Myth 3, Byrd and Bunting, in this volume.) Keeping these words visually accessible for students in a chart or table can facilitate their use and provide opportunities for illustrating use differences (such as the fact that *say* is more informal than *state*). Practice using reporting verbs, from tense exercises in low-intermediate classes to connotation and vocabulary work in advanced classes, helps reinforce the different forms.

- As memorization may be a familiar way of learning for ESL students, encourage students to sometimes use this practice and as a paraphrasing strategy. In order to retell or summarize information, ask students to reread selected material in a focused manner three times, put it aside, and then try to restate or write what they remember. Point out that on a first read, students understand; on the second and third read, they begin to internalize some of the words they will need for retelling. Often, the words they internalize are the content words. As they try to retell, they become aware of the need for function words (e.g., articles, prepositions, conjunctions) in writing as well as speaking. If students restate in writing, their texts can be compared (a) with each other and (b) with the original text for words and phrases in common. This activity increases awareness of essential elements to include in a paraphrasing or retelling, as well as which words or phrases might be "owned" by the original author.

- Translation of a selected text from English into a student's own language can also be used as a way to put a little distance between original words and a student's interpretation in order to retell or paraphrase. When translating, students internalize key concepts because they are interacting with the text. Then a retelling in English following a process similar to the one previously described can take place in written or spoken form.

10. **Integrate the use of citation with paraphrase and quotation across all levels of EAP writing (and speech and reading) in a program.**

   Even at beginning levels, students can work on including references to ideas or information gathered from others. Familiar sources such as people they know, famous people, or current topics in the news can be a starting point. First, work with reported speech should not be postponed until advanced levels. For example, conversations such as this can lead from informal to more formal written statements:

   > I heard that . . . XXX died.
   > Where did you hear that?
   > I heard it on the news.
   > According to a Channel 10 news report, XXX has died.
   > On Channel 10 today they reported that XXX has died.

   The same patterns can follow from *I read that* . . . to *According to XXX* . . .

   Elaboration can be scaffolded from these simple topic initiation points. Whatever topic is appropriate to a particular class and/or tied into a lesson, reporting what someone else has said or read about the topic is an opportunity for citation practice.

11. **Research institutional academic dishonesty policies and actual practice.**

   All colleges and universities have policies regarding plagiarism and cheating or copying. Helping students to become informed about this part of academic culture in an objective way can add to their sense of membership. Many institutions have an honor code, yet for most students new to the United States, the term *honor code* is not familiar. At intermediate or advanced levels, gathering information about institutional policies and practices can be part of a writing assignment. The first step is locating a current copy of relevant policy, perhaps in the student handbook, in the college catalogue, on the web, or through the student advisement office. Next, provide all of the students with copies and assign sections of the policies; small groups can then explain and summarize their findings, either orally or in writing.

For advanced students, interview tasks could be included. Students in small groups could make appointments to see various department chairs and student advisors to ask about plagiarism and about (anonymous) cases they have encountered. Initially, teaching interview skills is essential. Work with the students on the etiquette for making an appointment (or arranging an email interview), having a focused and limited set of questions, and following up with a thank you letter. Assign roles, such as researcher (a student responsible for knowing college policy, another student to learn about the administrator and find out about availability, etc.), interview/question leader, note-takers, and oral reporters for class debriefing. Then ask all of the students in the group to collaborate on a final written report of their findings or to work with in small groups to explain and summarize.

The job of teaching citation to ESL undergraduate students belongs to ESL teachers; we must acknowledge and address this student need as an important part of the writing curriculum in our writing programs. ESL students need to encounter authentic assignments; teachers can provide strategically planned exposure to, and systematic practice working with, the words of others in a spiraled curriculum strand specifically focused on citation conventions. Then our college students can feel confident about their inclusion in their general education courses. To benefit students the most, this work must begin early in a course of study and be revisited with regularity.

Questions for Reflection

1. As an undergraduate or a high school student, did you sometimes find it hard to differentiate between an effective way something you read was expressed and the way to use those techniques in your own writing? What was the outcome of your struggle?

2. If you were giving basic background information about a well-known person, how much of what you read, learned, or knew about that person is considered "common knowledge" that you could retell in your own language without a citation?

3. What strategies have you found successful in teaching writing students to paraphrase research material? What exercises or suggestions in this chapter might you add to your repertoire?

4. Rewriting curriculum for an EAP writing program to include early introductions to citation and reported speech may result in leaving some other technique or content out. If that is the case, what would you suggest be eliminated or reduced?

5. What options does the library associated with your ESL/EFL program offer to educate undergraduates in library research, online databases, and Internet searches? Have your writing class students participated in any of the materials or tours?

References

Abascal, J., Brucato, L., Stephenson, P., & Brucato, D. (2006). *Essential elements for effectiveness*. Boston: Pearson Custom Publishing.

Abasi, A., Akbari, N., & Graves, B. (2006). Discourse appropriation, construction of identities, and the complex issue of plagiarism: ESL students writing in graduate school. *Journal of Second Language Writing, 15*, 102–117.

The American heritage dictionary of the English language (4th ed.) (2007). Boston: Houghton Mifflin.

Cobb, T. (n.d.). Vocabulary profiler. *The Complete Lexical Tutor.* Retrieved September 21, 2007, from www.lextutor.ca/

Coxhead, A. (2000). A new academic word list. *TESOL Quarterly, 34*(3), 260–263.

Ercegovac, Z., & Richardson, J. V. (2004). Academic dishonesty, plagiarism included, in the digital age: A literature review. *College & Research Libraries, 65*(4) 301–318.

Pennycook, A. (1996). Borrowing others' words: Text, ownership, memory, and plagiarism. *TESOL Quarterly, 30*(2), 200–230.

Shi, L. (2006). Cultural backgrounds and textual appropriation. *Language Awareness, 15*(4), 262–282.

Wikipedia. (2007). Plagiarism. Retrieved April 30, 2007, from http://en.wikipedia.org/w/index.php?title=Plagiarism&oldid=133937159

3

Where Grammar Is Concerned, One Size Fits All

Pat Byrd and John Bunting
Georgia State University

In the Real World

WHILE OBSERVING ESL WRITING CLASSES, we have both had the experience of hearing teachers making statements to their students somewhat like the following . . .

> *Belief 1:* "Using passive voice is really bad writing. You should use active voice and lots of interesting active verbs in your writing."
>
> *Belief 2:* "Don't use the verb *to be*. Use more active verbs that will engage the audience."
>
> *Belief 3:* "Academic writers do not use *but* at the beginning of sentences. To be a good academic writer, you have to use a word like *however*."[1]

---

[1] More information is needed about the set of teacher beliefs about the language of academic writing. Numerous beliefs in addition to the pernicious effects of passive voice and the location of *but* seem to continue to be important to the belief systems of many writing teachers.

Analyses of large samples of academic writing have shown all three of these statements to be inaccurate as descriptions of academic prose. First, academic prose from a wide variety of disciplinary areas has been shown repeatedly to include frequent use of passive voice as part of the discourse style that values a focus on process and product rather than on the writer as actor (Biber, 1988). Second, such studies of academic prose also have demonstrated the limited range of verbs that are actually used; this relatively small set of verbs is repeated frequently within the context of sentences characterized by long, complicated noun phrases rather than by verb diversity. For example, the *Longman Grammar of Spoken and Written English* (Biber, Johansson, Leech, Conrad, & Finegan, 1999, p. 373) reports that

1. Twelve verbs are the most frequently used lexical verbs in the collection of English studied for that reference grammar: *get, go, make, come, take, give, know, think, see, want, mean, say.*[2] However, these twelve verbs are used repeatedly in conversation while only rarely used in academic writing.
2. In addition, conversation and fiction use a much greater variety of verbs than academic writing. For every million words of conversation, 120 different verbs are used; for fiction, 130 different verbs; for academic writing, about 80 different verbs.

The Biber et al. (1999, p. 65) reference grammar also found that academic prose is characterized by the use of about 300 nouns per million words along with 80 lexical verbs, 80 adjectives (to go with all of those nouns), and 40 adverbs (not many needed with so few verbs).

Third, in a study done for this chapter, the use of *but* was analyzed in the written academic texts collected by Coxhead (2000) for the

---

[2] The *Longman* corpus contains samples of conversational English, newspaper writing, academic prose, and fiction.

Academic Word List (AWL) project.[3] In that collection of approximately 3,000,000 words from academic texts, the word *but* is used only 159 times. Of these, 152 (96 percent) come at the beginning of the sentence. That is, while academic writers do not use *but* very often, when they do select that word, they are almost certainly going to put it at the beginning of a sentence.[4]

In this chapter, we analyze publications that give information about the language of academic writing and suggest resources that can be of use to teachers as they learn about the particular grammar and vocabulary characteristics of that academic writing. From this knowledge base, teachers can provide information, practice, and feedback that point their students toward appropriate use of English in their academic writing.

What the Research Says and Shows

Publications on grammar traditionally consider the structure of sentences and of words. . . . analyses usually termed *syntax* and *morphology*. Additionally, studies of grammar and vocabulary now often look at

---

[3] We are grateful to Averil Coxhead for providing the data for this small study. Because of copyright restrictions, she could not allow us to have access to the corpus but could provide the data needed to clarify the use of *but* in academic writing.

[4] The limited use of *but* in the AWL data supports the information provided by Biber et al. (1999) that *but* is more frequently used in conversation than in academic writing. At the same time, the use of *but* in academic writing demonstrates that discourse types are rarely pure and that academic writers can use *but* for specific purposes such as bringing an informal tone into their writing and when doing so generally violate the "rule" that the word should not be used at the beginning of a sentence. In approximately 16 percent of these uses of sentence-initial *but*, the authors seem to be making a stylistic choice by using the word in relatively short sentences such as the following, also often mimicking the language of conversation with the use of personal pronouns and questions:

But, asks Bayle, why not go further still?
But will the cabinet be smaller?
But a serious difficulty remains.
But I would never challenge someone on that basis.
But if we don't challenge, we become mute.

how language is used beyond the individual sentence or a single individual statement in a conversation. The term often used for these studies above the level of the sentence/word is *discourse.*

The Language Characteristics of Different Discourse Types ——

Through discourse studies, we learn how grammar and vocabulary are used for particular kinds of communication. Discourse can be conceived broadly as in the discourse of spoken English, or very narrowly, as in the discourse of classroom teachers in the language they use to ask questions in class; or broadly, as in the discourse of newspaper writing, or narrowly, as in the discourse of sports writing in U.S. newspapers; or broadly, as in the discourse of fiction, or narrowly, as in the linguistic characteristics of Shakespeare's tragedies.

Three samples of English are given in Figure 3.1 to illustrate how English differs according to communicative purpose. The first is a narrative from *The Outsiders* (Hinton, 1967), a work of fiction often read in high schools and also used in some IEPs; the second is a segment of an unrehearsed discussion among four students in a project work group from the MICASE corpus[5] (Simpson-Vlach & Leicher, 2006; Simpson & Swales, 2001); the third is from an undergraduate psychology textbook (Weiten, 1995).

FIGURE 3.1. Comparison of Three Samples from Different Discourses
Discourse Type #1

Fiction: From *The Outsiders* (Hinton, 1967).

> They walked out slowly, silently, smiling.
> "Need a haircut, greaser?" The medium-sized blond pulled a knife out of his back pocket and flipped the blade open.
> I finally thought of something to say. "No." I was backing up, away from that knife. Of course I backed right into one of them. They had me down in a second. I fought to get loose, and almost did for a second; then they tightened up on me and slugged me a couple of times. So I lay still, swearing at them between gasps. A blade was held against my throat.
> "How'd you like that haircut to begin just below the chin?"

---

[5] Unrehearsed conversation among students for a class project included in the MICASE corpus (2001).

Discourse Type #2

From an engineering project meeting that involved four students who were working on the budget for their project. There's a great deal of overlapping speech that can make the transcript a bit tricky to read but illustrates a major feature of interactive use of English. Speakers are labeled S1, S2, S3, and S4.

S1: we want one of those.

S2: <OVERLAP> what is it?

S3: <OVERLAP> one of what?

S1: i don't know but it's big.

EVENT DESCRIPTION="LAUGH"

S2: it's big

S3: it's probably big and expensive.

PAUSE

S2: well how are we doing on cost? i remember_ we didn't have a price for, water purification

S3: right or, the fermenter right?

S1: correct

S3: do you have that Zip disk?

S1: i do.

S3: you do, ya wanna pop it in (at least we'll,) see how we're doing, with cost?

S1: ["GROANS"]

S4: > (i think) we were up around a quarter million dollars weren't we?

S1: ["LAUGH"]

S2: yeah

S4: <OVERLAP> okay </OVERLAP>

S3: <OVERLAP> getting </OVERLAP> up there.

S1: fifty thou. (shucks.)

S3: i was just outside talking to like, who was out there, Ehon was out there and that other,

S3: how far along <OVERLAP> are they? </OVERLAP> Pratik, </OVERLAP> i think,

S1: ><OVERLAP> Pratik

S2: ><OVERLAP> Pratik is his name?

S2: > yeah

S1: > <OVERLAP> Pratik and, they were like oh, how are you doing? and i'm like oh we're getting there slowly but surely.

S1: are they outside?

S3: yeah outside

S1: <OVERLAP> i oughta say hello to them two

S3: wow

S4: how far along are they?

S3: <OVERLAP> must be nice, like they've,

S1: <OVERLAP> they ain't done nothing dude

Discourse Type #3

Academic prose, Psychology textbook sample (Weiten, 1995).

> Neurons are <u>individual cells in the nervous system that receive, integrate, and transmit information</u>. They are <u>the basic links that permit communication within the nervous system</u>. <u>The vast majority of them</u> are <u>interneurons - neurons that communicate only with other neurons</u>. However, <u>a privileged few, [called] sensory neurons</u>, receive <u>signals from outside the nervous system</u>. The entire nervous system depends on these specialized cells for <u>its information about lights, sounds, and other stimuli outside the body and about interior stimuli (a stomachache, for instance)</u>. Of course, <u>the plans of action [formulated] by the brain</u> must get from your brain to the muscles of your body. This communication [is handled] by motor neurons, which carry messages from the nervous system to <u>the muscles that actually move the body</u>.

While all three samples have nouns and verbs and other kinds of words along with combinations of words into units, the kinds of words and grammar used differ considerably.

- **Fiction** uses past tense verbs for much of the narrative line and for descriptive materials. A variety of descriptive words and phrases are used, including many adverbs to go with the many different active voice verbs and lots of adjectives to give the reader a sense of the characters and scene. Even when the writer attempts to mimic conversation language, the dialogue tends to be in fuller—with more diverse vocabulary and more grammatically complete, formal sentences—and less interactive overlapping language than in a live conversation like the one in the second part of Figure 3.1.

- **Conversation** uses highly interactive language: questions (and answers) come in short rather than grammatically complete forms; speakers understand some of the meaning from context rather than from a fully articulated statement; pronouns *I* and *you* are frequent along with lots of the useful noises that we make in conversation.

- **Academic prose** uses long complicated noun phrases with simple present tense verbs. The long complicated noun phrases often include prepositional phrases as well as relative clauses as post-modifiers of the core noun. Passive voice is widely used to keep the focus on processes and events rather than on actors.

An important observation for a composition teacher is that the forms and vocabulary used to create a piece of academic prose are not based on the grammatical forms and vocabulary used in conversational language or in fictional narratives.[6] Research publications (see Figures 3.3 and 3.4) report on the nature of various types of English and make it clear that English is not structured around a single unified set of grammar and vocabulary available for use in all communication settings.

English Grammar in Use

The grammar that is usually taught in ESL/EFL classrooms is a highly abstract conceptualization of English that seldom matches the real world use of English for communication. In that abstract version of English, verb tenses are explained with dictionary-type definitions while examples are often very short, un-contextualized creations of the textbook writer. Figure 3.2 quotes a typical ESL explanation of present tense verbs with a typical list of decontextualized examples. Being "typical" does not really excuse this approach that does not teach students how to use present tense in a conversation or in academic writing (as illustrated in the samples in Figure 3.1). The bracketed information identifies typical language settings/scenarios for such language use.

Research on English grammar shows that such a version of grammar is misleading when we want to know how English is used in real world communication. While such an approach to language and linguistics is useful for some theoretical linguists interested in human bio-psychology, the resulting language is not the language of communication. In fact, recent research into the characteristics of language-in-

---

[6] Certainly there are formats (email, postcards, letters to friends, written advertisements, and scripted speeches) when conversational language and written language overlap, but these newly emerging formats have their own linguistic accents that separate them from written academic prose and from face-to-face conversations.

FIGURE 3.2. Sample Grammar Definition and Examples from an ESL Grammar Website

Use the Simple Present to express the idea that an action is repeated or usual. The action can be a habit, a hobby, a daily event, a scheduled event, or something that often happens. It can also be something a person often forgets or usually does not do.

Examples:

- I **play** tennis.   [informal conversational setting]
- **Does** he **play** tennis?
- She **does** not **play** tennis.
- The train **leaves** every morning at 8 AM.   [more formal conversational setting.]
- The train **does not leave** at 9 AM.
- When **does** the train usually **leave**?
- She always **forgets** her purse.
- He never **forgets** his wallet.
- Every twelve months, the Earth **circles** the Sun.   [formal academic setting]
- **Does** the Sun **circle** the Earth?

Source: www.englishpage.com/webpage/simplepresent.html.

use gives us a quite different approach to English grammar of practical value for English-language teachers.

In the late twentieth century, computers became powerful enough and accessible enough for scholars to start building collections of English (for an overview see Biber, Conrad, & Reppen, 1998). These collections, which include mostly written English but also some transcriptions of spoken English, are called *corpora*. Often corpora are developed to investigate the language used in different types of English, such as newspaper English or academic writing or academic lectures or conversational English or some other discourse of interest to the scholar.

Books on English Grammar ——

Such studies of English grammar are published both in book formats (often as reference grammars) as well as in individual publications such as journal articles and book chapters in edited volumes. Following are findings from books that are useful for teachers investigating English grammar as it is used in context.

1. *Variation Across Speech and Writing* (Biber, 1988) used a statistical method called *factor analysis* to investigate a 500,000 word corpus[7]. The words in the corpus were tagged for grammatical categories and then a computer program analyzed which grammatical patterns tended to be used together frequently. The study reveals the types of grammar and vocabulary that tend to cluster in particular types of communication. Biber terms these clusters "the systematic patterns of linguistic [grammatical and lexical features] variation among registers" (for examples, see Biber, 2006, pp. 47, 86, and 252).

   Among the findings:

   > Academic prose tends to involve long complicated noun phrases, longer words (than in conversation), more different words than in conversation, passive voice, and complex sentences formed with participial clauses.

2. *Grammar in the Composition Classroom: Essays on Teaching ESL for College-Bound Students* (Byrd & Reid, 1998) applies corpus research such as that in Biber (1988) to teaching ESL composition and to issues in curricular design for ESL/EFL programs.

---

[7] For his 1988 study, Biber combined the Lancaster-Oslo-Bergen Corpus of British English (the LOB, a corpus of written English) and the London-Lund Corpus of Spoken English. While the corpus is small by current standards, the methodology and results remain valuable for insights into the complex of grammatical and lexical features that are characteristic of various discourses.

Among the findings:

Traditional ESL/EFL curricular design uses grammar in a way that distorts use of grammar in different types of communication. For example, traditional designs delay teaching of passive voice until advanced levels. However, passive voice is pervasive in scientific and technical writing, even at introductory levels of content for children and young students.

3. *The Longman Grammar of Spoken and Written English*[8] (Biber et al., 1999) is based on analysis of the Longman corpus as a whole, often with focus on particular subsets of the corpus. The four discourse types included are (a) newspaper writing, (b) conversation, (c) academic writing, and (d) fiction. This large reference grammar is based on empirical research and includes numerous findings about specialized usage in the different discourses studied.

Among the findings:

Traditional ESL/EFL grammar books just about always treat prepositions as (a) having independent meaning and (b) working in prepositional phrases for adverbial meaning. In that approach, a textbook might focus on the place meanings of *in*, *on*, and *at* used in sentences such as, *She lives in Atlanta on Springwood Drive* or *He lives in Decatur at 3335 NW 17th Street*. In contrast, studies of English-in-use show that prepositions often have close connections to verbs or nouns as with these phrases from the sample of academic writing given in Figure 3.1: *to carry something from somewhere to somewhere else* or a *vast majority of*. That is, prepositions often do not have

---

[8] The *Longman* has two valuable companion volumes: *The Longman Student Grammar of Spoken and Written English* (Biber et al., 2002a) and a workbook (Conrad et al., 2002) to go with that shorter version of the reference grammar. It should be noted that "student" does not mean "ESL learner" but more "those who would like to study English grammar to cultivate their own advanced knowledge of English," such as teachers and other scholars of English.

independent status but are part of very frequently occurring combinations of words. Also, prepositions are not used simply for the creation of prepositional phrases with adverbial meaning.

4. *Learning Vocabulary in Another Language* (Nation, 2001) discusses the conditions necessary for learning new vocabulary and for building the extensive vocabulary needed for academic study in a second language.

Among the findings:

- Grammar and vocabulary are highly interrelated and almost impossible to separate from each other without distortion of language-in-use.
- Learning a word involves learning more than its definition. To know how to use a new word, a learner must know about the grammatical patterns in which the word is most commonly used.

5. In *University Language,* Biber (2006) summarizes and expands on the analysis of academic language that he has published in numerous journals. After giving detailed information about various types of academic communication, he concludes with six fundamental patterns of academic communication (p. 213).

Among the findings: Biber shows that academic language in U.S. universities is characterized by:

- The pervasive differences between the linguistic features of academic speech and writing.
- The widespread importance of advising and classroom management language in both the speech of teachers and the written materials produced by the

university (that is, the widespread use of a common language for telling students what to do).

- Substantial language differences between the way instruction is handled in a textbook and by teachers in the classroom (where instructional content is mixed with interactive communication and classroom management talk).
- Language of "stance" or the expression of opinions and attitudes widely used even by teachers in classroom presentations and yet almost never used in textbook writing.
- Substantive language differences between the humanities and the social sciences on one end of a continuum and the hard sciences and engineering on the other end. Consequently, students will encounter substantially different ways of communicating in different disciplinary areas.

6. *Cambridge Grammar of English: A Comprehensive Guide. Spoken and Written English Grammar and Usage* (Carter & McCarthy, 2006) is a comprehensive English grammar reference book based on the 700 million-word Cambridge International Corpus (CIC), a collection of spoken and written English from the United Kingdom, the United States, and other parts of the English-speaking world.

Unlike other reference corpora, the CIC also includes a section on "learner English," samples of the language produced by ESL learners at various proficiency levels and carrying out a variety of communication tasks. The CIC also contains a subsection called CANCODE (Cambridge and Nottingham Corpus of Discourse of English), a corpus of spoken English developed by Cambridge University Press and the University of Nottingham. Because of the authors' interest in spoken English, special attention has been given to the grammar and pronunciation of English with the helpful addition of a CD that contains spoken examples to illustrate concepts presented in the printed version of the book.

The information provided throughout CANCODE about the characteristics of conversational English should be very useful for teachers of composition, especially with helping in the recognition of key grammatical and lexical differences between conversation and academic writing.

This information may be of special importance for teachers who are working with "ear learners" or with students who have learned much of their English through conversational interactions in U.S. settings rather than through formal instruction in non–English speaking countries (Reid, 2001, 2006). For composition teachers, these differences between conversational language and academic writing suggest strongly that students with high levels of spoken fluency and lower proficiency in writing cannot learn to write academic prose by working from their knowledge of conversational language and, indeed, will need to learn about features of language they may have rarely, if ever, encountered.

Among the findings:

- Spoken and written English are not two separate languages; they share vocabulary and grammar.
- However, the interactive language students hear and learn to produce in conversation can have features that are not appropriate for the highly planned and grammatically more complete sentences characteristic of academic prose. In an analysis of a sample of conversation (pp. 164–167), the authors demonstrate the features of spoken English, including:
  1. Communicative "units" are not like sentences but are generally shorter bursts of speech that can be single words or short phrases.
  2. Units that are presented as dependent clauses

in writing are used as independent units in speech. That is, units that teachers would mark as "fragments" are a regular feature of conversation. For example, adverbial clauses are often used as complete units in spoken English:

—<u>Speaker A</u>: "Why?"

—<u>Speaker B</u>: "Because I wanted to."

3. Pronouns that are contextually identified are frequently used (with more pronouns than nouns occurring in most conversations); that is, pronoun reference is clarified through shared information and context rather than linguistically.

4. Units tend to be shorter and include a more narrow range of vocabulary than written English.

Journal Articles and Book Chapters on English Grammar ——

Following is additional information from selected published studies about the use of English grammar in context.

1. Susan Conrad (2000) uses corpus linguistics to show how particular verbs are used with particular grammar. This information allows teachers to make informed choices about how to present materials depending on the speaking or writing situation encountered by ESL students. (See Myth 6, Conrad, in this volume for additional insights and information on the topic.)

   Among the findings: Conrad outlines three major changes that should occur in the teaching of ESL/EFL grammar:

   - A general grammar will be replaced by various register-specific grammars.
   - Grammar and vocabulary teaching will become more closely connected.
   - Emphasis will shift from grammatical accuracy to

identifying an acceptable range of choices for a specific setting.

2. Conrad (2004) discusses the relationships between language variation and corpus linguistics as it can be applied to language teaching. Variation refers to differences in the linguistic characteristics of different varieties of a language. For example, while both conversation and academic writing frequently use present tense, the lexical verbs in the two registers are considerably different.

Among the findings:

- "A lack of attention to variation can undermine teaching materials" (p. 70).
- The word *though* used as a linking adverbial is very common in speech, especially as a gentler way of showing disagreement (compared to *but* or *however*). The word is also often used at the end of an utterance. However, ESL textbooks usually don't provide information on this kind of lexico-grammatical variation.

3. In their investigation of academic discourse, Biber, Conrad, Reppen, Byrd, & Helt (2002) use a corpus-based multidimensional analysis to examine "a full range of registers encountered by students in university life" (p. 18). To examine the language used in U.S. universities, the authors used multidimensional analysis (Biber, 1988) to see how various linguistic features were operating together to serve a specific function, as opposed to looking solely at one feature at a time.

Among the findings:

- Spoken language and written language are different in academic discourse.
- Students encounter a wide range of language with

spoken and written discourse having substantial differences in both grammar and vocabulary.

- Students encounter much more interactive language in spoken English than might be initially assumed. Even lectures and other classroom speaking by teachers combine conversational interactive language with the more technical language that is featured in textbook writing and other academic prose.

4. Cortes' 2004 study analyzes lexical "bundles" (frequently recurring groups of words, sometimes called chunks or word combinations) in history and biology journals, and compares them to a range of student writing. The bundles identified in the history and biology journal articles are classified by structure and function, and then the use (or lack of use) of the bundles in the student writing is investigated.

Among the other findings:

- In both history and biology, many bundles were noun phrases + *of* (e.g., a *member of the, both sides of the*) and prepositional phrases + *of* (e.g., *as a result of, at the end of the*).

FIGURE 3.3. Differences in Bundles in History and Biology Articles

History	Many lexical bundles were used • referentially —as place markers —as quantifying bundles • as text organizers (e.g., comparison/contrast) • in framing (as in from *the perspective of*)
Biology	In addition to those used in History, "stance bundles" are used to express values and opinion (such as *it is possible that* and *are likely to be*).

Both the history and biology articles contained lexical bundles comprising
- noun phrases + *of* (e.g., a *member of the, both sides of the*)
- prepositional phrases + *of* (e.g., *as a result of, at the end of*)

- Many of the lexical bundles in the history corpus were used referentially (as place markers or as quantifying bundles) or as text organizers (contrast/comparison, or framing, as in *from the perspective of*). These same types of set phrases were also common in the biology corpus, along with "stance bundles" used to express values and opinions (such as *it is possible that* and *are likely to be*).
- About half of the lexical bundles identified in the journals were rarely used by student writers.
- The bundles students did use in history were often time markers, and in both history and biology, often the same student writer would use the same bundles at a much higher rate than in the published writing.

As a result of her findings, the author suggests that simple exposure to these lexical bundles may not be sufficient for learning to use them in writing because student writers were not using them in the same way as in the published writing, and sometimes overused certain lexical bundles.

5. Carter (2004) gives a shorter description of some distinct grammatical features of spoken conversational English, based on samples from CANCODE (see pp. 53–54). The issues are given longer treatment in the reference grammar book by Carter & McCarthy (2006).

Among the findings, Carter found that spoken language:

- uses phrases, sounds, and many incomplete clauses instead of the sentence as the basic structure.
- is based on a unit that is not the sentence but is a different type of structure that the author terms an *utterance*.

- requires a much different grammar than the grammar of written language.
- words that are unclassifiable using traditional grammatical labels, and there is less lexical linking between ideas, though through the use of gesture and sound, the conversation remains coherent.
- is characterized by interruptions, overlaps, and gestures, as well as by particular spoken language like that in Figure 3.1 (pp. 45–47).
- uses deixis (the use of body language) to point to people and things in the context where the conversation is taking place) (e.g., *Could we just move **that** into **this** corner **here?***)
- requires speakers to engage in a mutual construction of meaning, with many incomplete yet understandable structures.
- uses adverbs and adverb phrases that are more flexible in their placement than allowed in the grammar of written English (e.g., *You know which one I mean **probably***).
- uses vague language that softens or lessens specificity, a type of word choice that is often frowned upon in written English as sloppy or imprecise (e.g., *I don't want the suppliers complaining about it and stuff like that*).
- uses modal expressions to soften a message and to lower the degree of certainty or control (e.g., ***I don't know. I think** it's probably a change coming this way, **I suppose***).
- uses many clauses in a linear chain connected by conjunctions because speaking does not allow much time to plan utterances.

6. Eli Hinkel's *TESOL Quarterly* study (1995) shows how language use differs in principled ways among students from different cultural backgrounds. Specifically, the use of the modals for obligation and necessity in writing essays varied between NESs and NNSs of English.

Among the findings:

- NESs show more modals of obligation on the topic of racism, while some NNSs may direct that same force of obligation to the topic of family and tradition.
- NESs rarely used *ought to*, while NNSs used it frequently, perhaps showing that ESL textbooks do not include information about its primary use in spoken rather than written language.

7. Coxhead (2000) examines a corpus of academic writing and creates a list of 570 academic words (the Academic Word List or AWL) that occur frequently across many different fields with the focus on the disciplinary areas labeled *arts, commerce, law,* and *science.* The list excludes extremely common words from the General Service List (West, 1953) and divides the academic vocabulary into ten workable sublists of 60 words each (except the tenth sublist, which contains 30), based on frequency within the corpus. Each head word in the list actually represents a whole "family" of related words. For example, *require* is the headword for a word family that includes *require, requires, required, requirement, requirements, requiring.*

Among the findings:

- Academic language includes both highly common words from the 2,000 most common words in English along with other vocabulary more likely to be used in academic discourse.

- A piece of academic prose is made up of three types
  of vocabulary:
    a. words from the 2,000 most common words
       in English (West, 1953)
    b. highly specialized language found mostly in
       a particular discipline (e.g., proper nouns or
       special set terminology)
    c. academic words that are widely used in many
       different disciplinary areas (e.g., *percent, theory,*
       and *identification*)
- The highly frequent words on the Academic Word List
  are considerably less frequent in other types of texts,
  such as fiction. While the AWL words comprise 10
  percent of the Academic Corpus, they comprise less
  than 2 percent of a comparable corpus of fiction texts.

8. In Granger's 1999 study, she discusses ways to label words and
   phrases in a corpus so they can be categorized using corpus linguistics tools. Her focus is on using corpus linguistics methods
   to better understand the writing of EFL students. She and her
   colleagues have created a nine-category tagging system to label
   the errors that occur in a corpus of English language learner-
   produced texts.

   Using this tagged corpus, she investigates how error patterns shift between texts written by intermediate and advanced
   learners. Included are *formal, grammatical, lexico-grammatical,
   lexical, register, word redundant, word missing, word order,* and *style*
   (p. 192). Each of these categories has a number of subcategories
   (e.g., under *grammatical,* one subcategory is *verb tense errors*).

   Among the findings:

   - The verb tense errors that students made more fre-
     quently, which erroneous verb tenses were made,
     and the degree of accuracy in situations calling for
     each verb tense.

- The errors caused by student failure to look beyond the sentence level (in other words, the errors are not apparent when the sentence is decontextualized, but within the larger context the sentence is no longer correct).

Implications for Composition Teachers and Programs ——

These publications demonstrate that we do not have one single all-purpose grammar of English but several overlapping and interlocking grammars that are characterized by particular sub-sets of grammar and vocabulary. Most importantly to the context of teaching academic writing, the features of unrehearsed conversational spoken English are substantially different from those of formal revised written academic English, so different that some scholars are demonstrating that the basic structure of a conversation is not the sentence; they are also questioning the practice of analyzing the shorter forms used in conversation as reduced versions of written sentences. Thus, we would like to suggest that the myth is not just that "where grammar is concerned: one size fits all" but that it is a myth to think that "only one grammar exists." The true picture may be that "numerous related grammars exist." Moreover, the new data suggest even more strongly the importance of teaching students the differences between their conversational language and their academic writing: Academic writing is not conversation that has been written down.

What We Can Do

In her discussions of the teaching of grammar, Larsen-Freeman (2001) recommends the use of form-meaning-context not just to analyze grammar but also as a way to understand what we ourselves still need to know. In that same spirit of continuing to grow as teachers and grammarians, we offer these suggestions for (1) self-study by the teacher and (2) changes in content needed for lessons that will more effectively and efficiently prepare students to use the discourses that are important for their lives.

Issues in Teacher Knowledge and Study of English-in-Use ——

1. **Use a corpus-based dictionary for your own work as well as for your students**. One such dictionary is the *Macmillan English Dictionary for Advanced Learners* (Rundell, 2002). Another is the *Cobuild English Dictionary for Advanced Learners* (HarperCollins, 2001). The Macmillan dictionary provides a web-based version of the dictionary for those who have bought a copy of the book as well as teacher materials to use in teaching dictionary use with ESL/EFL learners. We would like to emphasize a major difference in dictionary use created by corpus-based dictionaries: In the past, probably the most important part of a dictionary entry was the definition with examples that frequently were not very useful. In contrast, readers of a corpus-based dictionary should focus on the examples to see authentic samples of how a word is used in context. The examples can even point to characteristic phrasing to help teachers (and then their students) learn how to use a word, moving away from abstract knowledge about "meaning" to concrete information about how to use a word for particular purposes in communication.

2. **Instruct your students on how to best use the various features in their corpus-based dictionaries**, including grammatical and lexico-grammatical information. The same comments given about teacher use of corpus-based dictionaries also applies to student use: focus must change from the definitions to the authentic examples of language in use provided with the definitions.

3. **Use a corpus-based grammar reference book to learn about the features of grammar and vocabulary that your students need to learn.** The two reference grammars listed on pages 50–55 (Biber et al. 1999; Carter & McCarthy, 2006) focus on the grammar and vocabulary really used for different types of communication and therefore are essential reading for ESL/EFL teachers.

4. **Do not learn your grammar solely from your ESL/EFL textbook.** Reach out beyond those sources to the scholarly works that are based on research into language-in-use. Current research results are expanding our knowledge about grammar and vocabulary. Teachers do not need to be the producers of this new knowledge, but they certainly should be the consumers, especially in using the highest quality reference tools for their selection of information to present in class.

Issues in the Design of Curricula, Lessons, and Materials ——

1. **Be clear about the reasons your students are studying English, and focus on the language that they need to achieve those purposes.** Find out the discourses that they need to use. For example, teachers can work with the textbooks and other assigned materials that are used in other classes their ESL students are taking (mathematics, psychology, political science, biology, and others) so that students learn the language they need for success in school.

2. **Learn what your students may know about how language varies with purpose and discourse, and help them to expand and apply that insight into language in use.** Many writing students, especially those who have lived for significant periods in the United States and received at least part of their education in U.S. public schools, are likely to be more familiar with conversational English than with written English. If they need to become fluent, accurate writers and readers of academic

English, they will need to recognize that language use changes with context and that academic language will require learning new vocabulary and new uses of grammar. Thus, students with particular educational backgrounds are likely to need help in learning to separate the language of conversation from the language of writing. The *Cambridge Grammar of English: A Comprehensive Guide. Spoken and Written English Grammar and Usage* (Carter & McCarthy, 2006) should be of great value in understanding the grammar and vocabulary of spoken English, providing insights that just were not available before this reference grammar was published.

To help students become consciously aware of how different grammar and vocabulary are used for various types of communication, students could, for example, become language detectives; they could learn to analyze, describe, and illustrate different registers of spoken English (in describing, for instance, how they might tell first a friend and then their grandmother about a party).

3. **When teaching writing, be sure to focus on the grammar and vocabulary most characteristic of the type of writing your students will need to produce.** Studying the language of fiction will not prepare students to handle the language of academic writing.

4. **Focus on the highly frequent in grammar and vocabulary.** Lists of the most frequent words in different types of communication can be found in many publications but perhaps most easily in reference grammars such as the *Longman Grammar of Spoken and Written English* (Biber et al., 1999) and the *Cambridge Grammar of English* (Carter & McCarthy, 2006). Corpus-based dictionaries generally also give information about the levels of frequency of words that they include.

5. **Connect vocabulary and grammar, and show students how to *notice* the connections and apply them to their own writing.** Working from lists of highly frequent vocabulary, teachers can

help students learn about the characteristic grammar of the words they are learning to use in their writing. For instance, students could learn to use a variety of highly frequent reporting verbs that require particular grammar, phrases such as *said that* or *reported on* or *suggested that.* Generally, such phrases require past tense, a subject that describes the source, and a clause or phrase in a particular form after the verb.

Again, the most efficient (as well as accurate and easily available) resources for teachers are corpus-based dictionaries and grammars. Paul Nation's work (2001) is particularly helpful in providing information on teaching and learning vocabulary within grammar contexts.

6. **Approach grammar and vocabulary not as individual, isolated features of English but as features of the particular discourses being studied by your students.** By working with grammar taken from specific contexts, teachers can be sure that they are teaching students how to use the language they are studying. That is, don't start with a list of grammar to teach; instead, start from the academic and disciplinary assignments that students will encounter, and then teach the language required for accurate communication in those registers.

For example, ESL/EFL teachers can provide reading passages characteristic of the materials that students must read in their other classes; indeed, they can take passages from the exact textbooks being used in required general education courses. Students can do a variety of language detective work such as underlining all the verbs, noticing the tenses being used, and starting their own lists of the verbs that are clearly important. Students can then analyze that same passage a second time, focusing on the noun phrases to see how these function in academic writing. They can return again and again to the same passage to look for the features of grammar and vocabulary characteristic of academic English and start to see how the grammar and vocabulary are part of a larger system.

Teachers need to consider what the students are learning about English vocabulary as well as English grammar. If the focus of a class is on academic language, then a teacher can prepare examples based on the textbooks that students are using for their classes. Or a teacher can find examples in the reading passages being used by the students in their other ESL/EFL classes.

In addition to ease of access and efficiency, one of the great values of corpus-based dictionaries is their use of real examples taken from the databases of language samples in the corpora that lie behind the dictionary entries. To use examples effectively, a teacher needs to plan ahead for the grammar (and vocabulary) that will be the focus of a class and to bring to students examples that show them how to use the grammar and vocabulary appropriately.

Questions for Reflection

1. One point made in this chapter is that you should focus on the grammar and vocabulary most characteristic of the type of writing your students will need to produce. For a group of students that you are working with (or are planning to work with), list characteristics of the language they are going to need to produce. How do you determine this list of characteristics?

2. Identify the key grammatical features that you want your students to notice for a specific course or unit. Using one of the grammar texts discussed in the text (Biber et al., 1999; Carter & McCarthy, 2006), select two or three of these features for examination. How is the feature addressed, and what information is different than in a traditional grammar text?

3. This chapter suggests focusing on highly frequent grammar and vocabulary patterns. For various groups of learners, how might you determine what those highly frequent patterns are? For one specific group, come up with several patterns that would be appropriate.

4. Consider you own knowledge as a user of English. Are there elements of grammar in ESL/EFL textbooks for which you feel you must provide qualification for your students? What are some elements that you disagree with, given your own experience, as both a teacher and speaker of English?

5. In considering the intersection of grammar and vocabulary, can you think of specific examples of these intersections for your students? In addition to the grammar resources mentioned in this chapter (Biber et al., 1999; Carter & McCarthy, 2006), what resources might you use to examine where grammar and vocabulary intersect?

References

Biber, D. (1988). *Variation across speech and writing.* Cambridge, UK: Cambridge University Press.

———. (2006). *University language.* Amsterdam: John Benjamins.

Biber, D., Conrad, S., & Leech, G. (2002). *Longman student grammar of spoken and written English.* Harlow, UK: Pearson Education.

Biber, D., Conrad, S., & Reppen, R. (1998). *Corpus linguistics: Investigating language structure and use.* Cambridge, UK: Cambridge University Press.

Biber, D., Conrad, S., Reppen, R., Byrd, P., & Helt, M. (2002). Speaking and writing in the university: A multidimensional comparison. *TESOL Quarterly, 36*(1), 9–48.

Biber, D., Johansson, S., Leech, G., Conrad, S., & Finegan, E. (1999). *The Longman grammar of spoken and written English.* Harlow, UK: Pearson Education.

Byrd, P., & Reid, J. (1998). *Grammar in the composition classroom: Essays on teaching ESL for college-bound students.* Boston: Heinle & Heinle.

Carter, R. (2004). Grammar and spoken English. In C. Coffin, A. Hewings & K. O'Halloran (Eds.), *Applying English grammar: Functional and corpus approaches* (pp. 25–39). London: Hodder Arnold.

Carter, R., & McCarthy, M. (2006). *Cambridge grammar of English: A comprehensive guide. Spoken and written English grammar and usage.* Cambridge, UK: Cambridge University Press.

Conrad, S. (2000). Will corpus linguistics revolutionize grammar teaching in the 21st century? *TESOL Quarterly, 34*(3), 548–559.

———. (2004). Corpus linguistics, language variation, and language teaching. In J. Sinclair (Ed.), *How to use corpora in language teaching* (pp. 67–85). Amsterdam: John Benjamins.

Conrad, S., Biber, D., & Leech, G. (2002). *Longman student grammar of spoken and written English: Workbook.* Harlow, UK: Longman.

Cortes, V. (2004). Lexical bundles in published and student disciplinary writing: Examples from history and biology. *English for Specific Purposes, 23,* 397–423.

Coxhead, A. (2000). A new academic word list. *TESOL Quarterly, 34*(2), 213–238.

Granger, S. (1999). Use of tenses by advanced EFL learners: Evidence from an error-tagged computer corpus. In H. Hasselgard & S.

Oksefjell (Eds.), *Out of corpora: Studies in honour of Stig Johansson* (pp. 191–202). Amsterdam: Rodopi.

HarperCollins Publishers. (2001). *CoBuild English Dictionary for Advanced Learners.* New York: HarperCollins Publishers.

Hinkel, E. (1995). The use of modal verbs as a reflection of cultural values. *TESOL Quarterly, 29*(2), 325–343.

Hinton, S. E. (1967). *The Outsiders.* New York: Penguin.

Larsen-Freeman, D. (2001). Teaching grammar. In M. Celce-Murcia (Ed.), *Teaching English as a second or foreign language* (3rd ed.) (pp. 251–266). Boston: Heinle & Heinle.

Nation, P. (2001). *Learning vocabulary in another language.* Cambridge, UK: Cambridge University Press.

Reid, J. (2001). Writing. In R. Carter & D. Nunan (Eds.), *The Cambridge guide to teaching english to speakers of other languages* (pp. 28–33). Cambridge, UK: Cambridge University Press.

———. (2006). *Essentials of teaching academic writing.* Boston: Houghton Mifflin.

Rundell, M. (Ed.) (2002). *Macmillan English dictionary for advanced learners.* Oxford, UK: Macmillan.

Simpson, R. C., & Swales, J. (2001). *Corpus linguistics in North America: Selections from the 1999 symposium.* Ann Arbor: University of Michigan Press.

Simpson-Vlach, R., & Leicher, S. (2006). *The MICASE handbook: A resource for users of the Michigan corpus of academic spoken English.* Ann Arbor: University of Michigan Press.

Weiten, W. (1995). *Psychology: Themes and variations.* Belmont, CA: Brooks Cole (A Thompson Learning Company).

West, M. (1953). *A general service list of English words.* London: Longman.

Make Your Academic Writing Assertive and Certain

Ken Hyland
Institute of Education, University of London

In the Real World

NON-NATIVE STUDENTS OF ENGLISH OFTEN approach academic writing assignments with the idea that they have to be definite and self-assured. They have been taught that academic writing should be a strong expression of ideas and that any fuzziness or uncertainty muddies clear argument and effective style. Even students with fairly advanced levels of English and a good grasp of the grammar and vocabulary they need to communicate effectively can find navigating the tricky waters of essay writing a perilous experience, especially when they tend to see English as a direct and uncompromising sort of language, intolerant of detours and unforgiving of vagueness. The instruction to avoid hedges is, however, another writing myth, and perhaps the most persistent and misleading one in academic writing.

In spite of the fact that ESL/EFL students believe native English speakers are "direct" and "assertive," those characteristics are, in cultural reality, a matter of degree. A **hedge** is a word or phrase used frequently to qualify statements. In spoken English, hedges like *I think* and *maybe* allow us to express an opinion without demanding that our listeners accept the opinion as a fact. For example, statements such as **I think** *cricket is a better game than baseball* and **Maybe** *we should go to the beach this weekend* offer listeners the option of rejecting the idea and giving their own. This is one reason for using tag questions such as, *That's an excellent film,* **isn't it?** and *I love those shoes,* **don't you?** as they involve listeners more by giving them a chance to respond.

Hedges are therefore considered polite because they don't force our conversational partners into a corner. In contrast, unqualified assertions such as, *Daycare should be free to all parents* and *Republicans don't care about the poor* may actually seem aggressive to the listener, rather than simply assertive. In fact, these kinds of statements are likely to be counter-productive if we are trying to persuade people to agree with us; we may actually end up alienating them.

Academic writing is no less persuasive than talking, and hedges are just as important. For students, being a credible writer in large part means persuading a teacher, tutor, supervisor, or examiner that they understand the subtleties, nuances, and complexities of an idea and that others might have different views than one's own. This is where hedges can help. In English academic writing, writers use hedges to express levels of doubt and certainty—that is, to express their level of confidence—about the topic they are investigating. One reason for hedging is to offer an opinion about the accuracy of the material being used; another is to connect with the reader, offering the reader an opportunity to evaluate that material. While writers in the sciences tend to draw on a different subset of items than those in the humanities, the ten most frequently used hedges in professional academic writing are:

assume	*could*	*indicate*	*likely*	*may*
might	*possible(ly)*	*seem*	*suggest*	*would*

In short, hedging is a culturally accepted and expected persuasive technique in academic writing.

However, the term *hedging* tends to have negative connotations in written academic language. Students are often taught to argue confrontationally, competitively, and antagonistically in debating clubs across the United States, while numerous writing textbooks and style guides state that hedging indicates equivocation and perhaps even deviousness. Many types of teaching materials insist that writers avoid all tentativeness in their writing and instead speak plainly, arguing that hedging robs writing of its certainty and power, undermining the persuasiveness of the argument. Hedging is seen as padding and wasteful, as in this advice from a style guide:

> If you have no conclusive evidence don't dither around with expressions such as "it may be possible that" or (worse) "the possibility exists that . . . ," which immediately suggests that you do not believe your own data. (Lindsay, 1984)

Perhaps more eloquently, *The Elements of Style,* often required reading for American high school and college composition classes, calls hedges "the leeches that infest the pond of prose, sucking the blood of words" (Strunk & White, 2000, p. 12). Heady stuff!

The ubiquity of such advice suggests that many teachers accept the myth and bring it into their teaching, telling students to avoid reticence and advising them to stick to supportable facts. In a final-year Hong Kong secondary school classroom, for instance, I watched a teacher introduce a worksheet that advised students to use this list of expressions for introducing statements in essays:

It cannot be denied that	*As we all know*	*As you know*
In fact	*As a matter of fact*	*I feel that this is*
There is no doubt that	*I think that the*	*I do believe that*
As we can see	*It is true that*	*I do not agree with*

Because the general view is that English is a direct, no-nonsense language, learners tend to produce sentences such as these, taken from Hong Kong student exam scripts:

> Indeed, **there is no doubt** that reading comic books can reduce an extreme high pressure among students and **in fact will definitely** improve their English.

> **Of course, as we all know, it is certain** that students are attracted to the brand name fashions and **always** find a part-time job after school to buy them.

> **In fact, you must know** that Hong Kong is a wealthy city and it is **certain** that it will continue to develop prosperously.

But while both oral debates and academic statements have to carry the writer's conviction, claims like these can seem too blunt, rigid, and even aggressive to many academic readers. The myth is beginning to crack.

What the Research Says and Shows

Hedging research is often based on the analysis of hundreds of student papers (hundreds of thousands of words) that are stored in a computer as a corpus. By using concordance software, researchers can search such a corpus for hedges to find how frequently different forms are used and how they are used. For example, it is possible to isolate every instance of *suggest* and find out its tense, whether it is usually active or passive, and what words it might be commonly associated with. I have used corpora of academic articles, textbooks, and student writing for my work, searching them for hedges. For instance, in one study with John Milton (Hyland & Milton, 1997), we used a collection of 900 essays (500,000 words) written by Hong Kong students and a corpus of

500,000 words written by British school-leavers of similar age and education level. Both corpora were examined for a list of 75 of the most frequently occurring lexical expressions of doubt and certainty. (For further discussion of corpus-based research, see the Byrd & Bunting and the Conrad chapters in this volume.)

How Frequent Are Hedges? ——

Hedging research has demonstrated that experienced academic writers, such as academics and successful native speaker writers, use a hedge about one word in every 50 on average, or one every two or three sentences. Interestingly, this figure is only slightly less than that for the use of passive voice and past tense verbs (Hyland, 1998a). We also know that we are far more likely to find hedges in writing in humanities and social science essays than in natural science and engineering subjects, mainly because writers in the humanities and social science fields are usually less certain about their results and have to hedge both to protect themselves against being wrong, and to show that they respect readers' possible alternative opinions about issues (Hyland, 1998a, 1988b, 1994).

Research also shows us which hedges we are most likely to find in academic writing, and, therefore, which might be most useful to teach. In fact, hedges include a bewildering array of potential hedging words and phrases from across different grammatical categories, and they express a range of different strengths of hedging. In addition, writers often use hedges in clusters, combining several hedges to strengthen the force of the hedge. Expressions such as *it might be possible* and *it seems likely that* are very common in academic genres (Hyland & Milton, 1997). Consequently, it might be useful to teach some hedging phrases in clustered patterns. Figure 4.1 lists some commonly used hedges in a variety of word classes as well as the general comparative strengths of those items.

FIGURE 4.1. Some Hedges, Their Categories, and Their Strengths

Word/Phrase		Grammar Category	Usual Strength/Weakness
			certain doubtful <———————>
Most Common	It may be possible	modal + adjective	<————————X—>
	might	modal	<————————X—>
	would	modal verb	<——X————>
	probably	adverb	<———X————>
Fairly Common	I believe	hedging lexical verb	<——X————>
	It is extremely unlikely	adverb + adverb	<————————X—>
	It seems	hedging lexical verb	<——X————>
	The results suggest	hedging lexical verb	<—X————>
Less Common	estimate	modal noun	<———X————>
	perhaps	adjective	<————————X——>
	possibility	modal noun	<—————————X—>

It is worth noting that a number of the words in these hedges are among the highest frequency words in academic writing and are certainly far more numerous than many other items that usually get much more attention in academic writing courses. Examples such as these are familiar to readers of academic texts:

> I think it is **likely that** this is due to poor weather.

> It **seems possible that** the findings **may be** influenced by sampling errors.

> **The results suggest that** there is no relationship between the two.

> Krashen **claims that** this is due to the operation of the affective filter.

Why Hedge? ——

Frequency is, of course, a good reason for teaching language items because we can predict that those items are likely to be useful to students. But unlike many frequently used vocabulary words (e.g., *nice, very, thing, like*), hedges occur frequently for important rhetorical reasons. Basically, research demonstrates that **hedges express three important functions: to express precision, to protect the writer against being wrong, and to show the writer's modesty or respect for readers** (Hyland, 1998a). These reasons—precision, protection, and politeness—often overlap, but it is still useful for students to identify which reason is being used and to discuss the effects each hedge has on readers.

1. **Hedges allow writers to express themselves more precisely.**
   While hedges in everyday terms might be associated with fuzziness and ambiguity, in academic writing they allow writers to express their ideas and opinions with greater accuracy. As teachers, we know the importance of interpretation and judgment in research writing, as well as the specification of the actual state of knowledge. Far from always being certain and definite, ideas and research findings are often speculative, uncertain, and open to question. Hedges allow writers to convey these levels of certainty/uncertainty (i.e., the actual state of knowledge) more clearly. Often, for example, it is far more precise to say *X may cause Y* than to use the more definite *X causes Y*. Students can learn to convey the differences between (a) certain knowledge, (b) plausible reasoning, and (c) supposition with appropriate hedges. These student sentences use hedges to convey the uncertainty of their conclusions effectively:

   - This **suggests** that there **may be** a connection between reading comics and improved grades.
   - Comics **seem to** develop students' interests in reading and **might** lead them to read stories.

2. **Hedges allow writers to head off challenges to their ideas.**
   While composition textbooks state that students must make the strongest possible points and arguments, the students also need to protect themselves against overstatement and overconfidence by limiting their claims to what they can reasonably support. Research shows that the more assertive the statements in academic student writing, the more material is needed to support it, and the more likely readers are to challenge the ideas or opinions. Hedges help writers avoid making too much of a commitment to their statements and allow them to present an idea in a more cautious and circumspect way (Hyland & Milton, 1997).

   A liberal sprinkling of hedges means that student writers are able to show that they are sensitive and perceptive enough to recognize the limitations of their point of view and to be cautious about what they are claiming. One common way writers protect themselves from the possible dangers of a categorical assertion is to express themselves using a non-agentive "evaluative *that* structure" with a hedge, replacing a personal subject with a *dummy "it"* or an inanimate source (Hyland & Tse, 2005), as in these phrases:

Somewhat Cautious	More Cautious
it seems that . . .	*data suggest that...*
it appears that . . .	*the model implies that . . .*
it is likely that. . . .	*newspaper reports indicate that. . . .*

3. **Hedges allow writers to project an honest and modest persona that helps them build connections with their readers.**
   Similar to the ways that we hedge in casual conversation, reducing the force of our arguments to be polite increases the chances of persuasion, of getting an opinion accepted. In contrast, firm, unhedged assertions may clearly state what we think, but they leave no room for discussion or doubt and imply that the lis-

tener's or reader's views are not worth considering. Offering a strident unqualified categorical assertion can threaten readers and therefore be unpersuasive because the reader/listener is automatically assigned a passive, accepting role.

Instead, students who preface statements with a hedge and refer to themselves as the source of the statement show readers that the writers' ideas and opinions are personal views. For example, by adding the bold faced hedges in these examples, the students were able to convey that they intended their ideas to be taken as possibilities, an alternative among many, rather than a definitive statement of truth.

> **Personally, I believe that** comic books are very useful if they are used for educational purposes.
>
> **For this seems to suggest to me that** we don't need the royal family.
>
> **I suggest** we need to watch American films to improve our English.

Why Do L2 Writers Find Hedges Difficult to Use? ——

The ability to express qualification and doubt appropriately in English academic writing is a complex task for L2 writers. Research demonstrates that, in fact, non-native speakers of English frequently give the same direct and unqualified weight to accepted fact and unsupported assumptions. For example, Chinese and Hong Kong students often employ a more direct tone and make unjustifiably strong assertions when they write in English (Hyland & Milton, 1997), while Japanese and Korean students often overhedge and exhibit what English-speaking readers see as hesitancy and uncertainty (Hinkel, 2000). The reasons for these difficulties are complex but are at least partly because a single hedging expression can convey a range of meanings. Many modal verbs, for instance, can express a range of different senses, as we can see from the brief examples in Figure 4.2:

FIGURE 4.2. Main Senses of Modal Verbs

Modal	Possibility (Hedge)	Logical Possibility	Permission	Ability	Obligation	Prediction
can		X	X	X		
could	X	X		X		
may	X	X	X			X
might	X	X				
should	X	X			X	
would	X	X				X

A second reason for student difficulties is that hedging can be expressed in a large variety of ways; Holmes (1988), for example, believes that at least 350 devices are potentially available for this purpose.

A third reason ESL/EFL student writers have difficulties with appropriate hedging is the poor advice they get from their English language textbooks, which tend to either ignore or misrepresent their importance. In a survey of 22 popular ESL/EFL writing textbooks a few years ago, for example, I found that students are often not taught alternatives to categorical assertions (1994), and so they do not look for ways to moderate their arguments. Further, students are not likely to find many examples of hedges in their academic textbooks because these tend to present information as facts rather than possibilities (Myers, 1992).

A final reason why L2 learners may have problems with hedging is cultural. Speakers of different languages express arguments and hedge in rhetorically different ways. Academic writing in German and Czech, for example, seems to be more direct than writing in English (Bloor & Bloor, 1991), while Asian writers are said to be influenced by Confucian rhetorical styles that value greater hedging and diffidence. Further, Arabs, Finns, Japanese, Malays, and Chinese seem to prefer more cautious and indirect argument patterns than we typically expect in English (Hinkel, 2002). Because students may have a good idea of lexical and grammatical differences between their home language and English, they may be unaware of what counts as appropriate formality, directness, deference, and other pragmatic rules that operate in English academic settings.

A summary of some key results from the hedging research is shown in Figure 4.3.

FIGURE 4.3. Summary of Some Key Research on Hedging

Study	Among the Findings
Fahnestock, J. (1986) Studied how the same scientific claims are expressed differently in research reports and popular science articles.	1. Extensive hedging in research articles underscores the uncertainty of experimental results. 2. Change in audience results in removal of hedges in popular science articles to present ideas as facts.
Myers, G. (1992) Explored the use of hedging to present information in subject textbooks.	1. Textbooks present claims as accredited facts. 2. Hedges mainly refer to matters not yet agreed upon. 3. Students only familiar with textbooks will be unable to use the hedges effectively in academic writing.
Hyland, K. (1994) Examined 22 popular international EFL textbooks at different proficiency levels for their advice on hedging	1. Poor coverage of hedging overall. 2. Concentration only on modal verbs. 3. Minimal coverage of adverbs, nouns, and hedging adjectives.
Hyland, K., & Milton, J. (1997) Examined a computer corpus to compare the expressions of doubt and certainty in written examinations of Cantonese and British students of similar age and education level.	1. L2 writers use far stronger commitments (by overstating and using assertive structures). 2. L2 writers exhibited greater problems conveying a precise degree of certainty or doubt. 3. Both groups depended heavily on a narrow range of items, principally modal verbs and adverbs.
Hyland, K. (1998a) Detailed study of forms and functions of hedging in biology articles.	1. Hedges used for 3 main purposes are each expressed in many different ways. 2. Most common hedges are lexical verbs and adverbs, followed by adjectives, modal verbs, and then nouns. 3. Hedges are also expressed syntactically as questions, conditionals, etc.
Hyland, K. (1998b) Corpus study of certainty (boosters) and hedges in 56 research articles in 8 disciplines.	1. Hedges outnumber "boosters" 3:1 and occur every 49 words. 2. Humanities social science disciplines use hedges about 2.5 times more than science and engineering fields.

What We Can Do

Academic reading and writing are integral to teaching hedging devices. We need to help learners to distinguish facts from interpretations when they read and to identify a range of high-frequency hedges used effectively in academic writing. Students need to learn how to use hedging strategies and then have multiple opportunities to practice using hedges appropriately.

We need to start teaching hedging strategies at early stages of language and writing proficiency because hedges are a key part of learning how to write effectively, not an optional extra to be added later when other things have been mastered. I should emphasize that while even beginning students should be taught hedges, we need to provide as much support as possible in the early stages. Using readings as examples and modeling appropriate levels of certitude are good ways to begin teaching hedges. Students may then discuss in pairs or small groups the strengths of claims during drafting and revising sessions.

Some techniques and sample exercises that have been effective with my students follow. The teaching suggestions I outline here move the learner from awareness to recognition to understanding and finally to use.

1. **Teach common and productive forms.**

   To be successful, students not only need to identify and understand hedges but to actively use them in their writing. We therefore should select those items for teaching that are both frequent and productive—that is, found across a range of different academic text types. By concentrating on the most frequent hedges, we can offer students the best returns for the least learning effort, especially in the early stages of writing. (See Figure 1 above for a list of the most frequently used hedges.) Further, the most productive items give students control over hedges that can be used in the greatest variety of patterns or combined with other items in useful collocations. Because both modals and lexical verbs are often used together with other hedges, this allows devices to be introduced and learned in patterned phrases like these:

This might suggest that . . .   It seems likely that . . .
I believe it is possible that . . . We think it might be possible . . .
I assume this might . . .   This may indicate that . . .

Finally, learning hedging items in context will help students to recognize a high proportion of the hedges they are likely to come across in their reading and to moderate their statements effectively when they write. Concentrating on a few items can help learners make their writing more subtle and at the same time can also foster familiarity with the concepts of hedging.

2. **Raise awareness of hedging forms.**

   Teachers can help students even with low-intermediate academic writing skills to understand the effects of hedges with tasks that focus on short texts or text extracts. Several sample activities follow.

   a. Examine a text, and distinguish statements that carry the writer's certainty and those where the writer is uncertain by marking them with C (certain) or U (uncertain):

      Example:

      - There is no answer to this.   (C)
      - In such cases, the press appear to have forced
        unnecessary actions.   (U)
      - This is likely to cause resentment in the poorer
        communities.   (U)
      - The trends from overseas invariably affect
        Hong Kong people.   (C)

   b. Identify all the hedges in a text by circling the forms used, and then discuss why writers may have hedged at those points, drawing on the three possible reasons for hedging discussed: hedging for (a) **precision**, (b) **protection**, or

(c) **politeness**. While it is not always possible to be sure about a writer's reasons for hedging, the discussion will help raise students' awareness of the issues.

Example:

- *It seems likely that* (**precision**) this was the result of temperature changes.
- Firstmore *might* (**protection**) be different not only in its chromosomal arrangement but also in displaying a particular mechanism.
- This *may* (**politeness**) have important implications for further research.

c. Locate and remove all the hedges from a text; then discuss the effect this has on the meaning of the text.

d. Identify hedged statements in a text, and substitute them with statements of certainty; then discuss the differences in tone.

e. Identify hedges in a text, and decide what effect they have on each statement on a scale of probability to possibility.

f. Consider whether hedges vary in their meaning across languages by asking students to translate hedged sentences into their L1.

3. **Assign rewriting tasks.**
A number of rewriting tasks can encourage students to begin to use hedges productively, and these can be modified for users of different language proficiency and stage of education. Following are sample exercises.

a. **Low-intermediate to high-intermediate writers:** Students can rework the abstracts or titles from journal articles in their specific fields by the addition or subtraction of hedges so the certainty of these texts is affected.

b. **Intermediate to advanced student writers:** Provide statements from newspapers, textbooks, or other everyday sources, and ask students to rewrite them. In this rewriting they should either include or omit hedges to change the degree of certainty of the statements.

Example:

> 15 more people were ~~reported to have been~~ arrested in Pakistan. Known militants already serving sentences ~~are also understood to have been~~ *were* interviewed in Pakistani prisons. The majority of the arrests ~~appear to have taken~~ *took* place in the Punjab region over the past two days. Prisoners in jails in Karachi and Rawalpindi were ~~reported to have been~~ interviewed although the Pakistan government has so far released little information on the arrests. Most attention is still focused on a Briton, Rashid Rauf, who was arrested in Pakistan and has been described by authorities in Pakistan and the UK as a key player in the ~~alleged~~ plot.

c. **High-intermediate to advanced writers:** Students can be asked to reformulate a textbook passage from the perspective of a scientist presenting the ideas for the first time in a research report, making the claims more tentative. This introduces students to the idea that texts have different audiences and purposes and that hedges are an important way of responding to these different circumstances.

d. **Advanced writers:** Provide students with a text of experimental results or a claim from their own discipline and ask them to paraphrase the main results, writing a list or description that uses hedges to express the cutting-edge uncertainty of the claims.

4. **Provide opportunities for longer writing tasks.**
L2 students often have difficulty evaluating reader expectations and what readers are prepared to accept, so they need opportunities to develop strategies for varying the strength of claims for particular purposes and readers. Paragraphs or essays that

require students to argue a position in a debate, speculate on likely causes for events, or hypothesize about future possibilities are obvious means of focusing attention on appropriate uses of hedges.

Students can be encouraged to consider their statements and audience, draw on their own subject knowledge, and employ a range of hedges appropriately. Some tasks that have worked well for me in the past:

a. Set free-writing activities that require students to explore personal histories and to speculate on possible alternative directions and life choices at certain points in the past or on possible different options for the future.

b. Give students a polemical editorial or account of a political speech from a newspaper and ask them to write a rebuttal—a letter to the editor or an essay. The student text should be measured and cautious, using hedges where necessary to soften the impact of the arguments on readers and to convey caution about uncertain information.

c. Assign an essay or a discussion section of a research paper that encourages students to make hypotheses about future possibilities from graphs, statistical trends, experimental results, etc. Less proficient students might be asked to speculate about "what might happen next" based on a photograph, a paused video segment, or a series of cartoon drawings.

d. Provide students with essay topics that call for speculation and conjecture to encourage the use of hedging in expressing cause and effect connections, reasons, or potential outcomes. Liberal arts topics such as the reasons for inflation, drug abuse, university dropout rates, juvenile crime, and so on usually work well.

e. Ask students to contribute a short essay for a class journal/magazine about the state of knowledge on a topic or the implications of a new development or finding in the student's discipline. The fact that the claims are new and readers unaware of them should encourage plenty of hedging.

5. **Encourage contrastive reflection.**

   A good way to start with learners who are fairly proficient and experienced academic writers is to encourage them to reflect on how they hedge in their first languages. For example,

   > *Example.* Present students with a series of example sentences in English and ask them to place a checkmark (✔) where they might use a hedge in their L1 academic writing. Then, in a class discussion, provide appropriate English hedges and discuss why their L1 patterns and academic English may differ. Such contrastive analysis and reflection is useful for helping students to see how different languages have different—not better or worse—conventions for expressing ideas. Students might then discuss how they might adapt to the English academic hedging style.

6. **Promote research of hedges.**

   Teachers can give intermediate and advanced learners small projects that focus on hedging in their own disciplines or subject areas. Relating tasks to students in this way means students can use their developing linguistic competence and subject knowledge in a context of immediate relevance to them.

   > *Assignment.* Select two or three articles from an international journal or other periodical in your field; photocopy those articles. Highlight the hedges in each article with a colored pen, then count and categorize your findings, either by the form of the hedge (noun, modal, adverb) or by its likely function (precision, protection, politeness). You will then use these results to present to the class in the form of a graph.

   > *Example.* Students might form groups to pool their expertise and discuss similarities and differences in their findings. Or, individual students or the small groups might draft an essay or give a presentation on their findings. Or, this task can be extended so that undergraduate students, working in groups, develop sets of interview or survey questions to ask their course instructors about hedging in their disciplines and their own writing practices.

7. **Support corpus exploration.**

Another approach is to encourage students to study a corpus of texts using a computer concordancer. A concordance program is a tool for searching large amounts of computer-readable text for particular words and combinations, but while it can isolate, sort and count data, the actual analysis is performed by humans. Gathering data with a concordancer can be done quite easily by students themselves by using an online concordance resource such as that available at the Virtual Language Centre (VLC) site at *www.edict.com.hk/concordance/* or the Cobuild Direct site at *www.collins.co.uk/corpus/CorpusSearch.aspx.*

Both these sites are user-friendly with help screens and simple-to-use interfaces, making it easy for both students and teachers who may be new to concordancing. While not all teachers are familiar with this methodology, it can offer effective pedagogic opportunities and really holds no perils for adventurous instructors wanting to add a new approach to their repertoire.

Students can also participate in corpus exploration. Essentially, this approach allows students to engage independently with the language by searching for individual items or strings of words provided by the teacher in relevant collections of authentic texts. This allows them to identify the most common hedges and, by looking at the surrounding text (or **collocations**), to discuss how the hedges are used and the strength of commitment they convey.

> *Assignment.* Go to the VLC Web Concordancer at: *www.edict.com.hk/concordance/.* Select a corpus in the "English—Simple search" screen, and type in the word *possible* (to search for). Now answer these questions:
>
> - How many times does the word *possible* occur?
> - Is it mainly used as a noun or an adjective?
> - How many times is it used as a hedge?
> - Can you see any difference in meaning between *possible to, possible for,* and *possible that?*
> - Now search for the words *likely, seem, probably, suggest,*

might, and *could.* Compare their frequencies and the words they most frequently occur with.

While many L2 students believe they must always be direct and assertive in English, this turns out to be another myth about English academic writing. Teaching ESL/EFL writing students how to hedge appropriately should be a priority for EFL writing teachers. We need to recognize that students often have serious problems with achieving an appropriate balance of conviction and assertion in their writing, but that providing them with the language they need to express themselves more delicately can have a huge payoff by transforming blunt and dogmatic prose into scholarly and sensitive reflection. That is, the use of hedges at appropriate points in students' texts can have immediately positive effects by showing that the writers are aware of alternative possibilities to their claims, that they respect their readers' viewpoints, and that they are modest enough to present their ideas with caution.

Questions for Reflection

1. Some teachers ignore the role of hedges in their teaching, arguing that writing is complex enough without adding more to teach. How would you respond to this argument?

2. Collect some reference materials such as style/reference guides, rhetorics, student writing manuals, and ESL and NES grammar books (either print or electronic). Read what they have to say about hedging. Are the texts consistent in the information and degree of importance they give to hedging? How far does the information or advice agree with your own knowledge or ideas on the issue? Consider whether or not you might make use of this information in a writing class.

3. Hedges encourage us to consider both what we say and who we say it to. Write a brief argument for the introduction of higher student fees or banning alcohol on campus for a student newspaper. What aspects of the text suggest that the (student) audience might be opposed to your ideas? How might your hedges work to persuade them?

4. Collect all the mail that arrives at your home for one week. Now do a brief survey of hedging by counting all the items which seem to function to tone down the strength of the text. Can you categorize the hedges that you find (as precision, protection, or politeness), in the ways they were used and the types of text where you found them? What conclusions can you draw from this about the use of hedges in everyday writing?

References

Bloor, M., & Bloor, T. (1991). Cultural expectations and socio-pragmatic failure in academic writing. In P. Adams, B. Heaton, & P. Howarth (Eds.), *Socio-cultural issues in English for academic purposes. Review of ELT* (pp. 1–12). Basingstoke, UK: Modern English Publications/British Council.

Fahnestock, J. (1986). Accommodating science: The rhetorical life of scientific facts. *Written Communication, 3*(3), 275–296.

Hinkel, E. (2002). *Second language writers' texts.* Mahwah, NJ: Lawrence Erlbaum.

Hyland, K. (1994) Hedging in academic writing and EAP textbooks. *English for Specific Purposes, 13*(3), 239–256.

———. (1998a). *Hedging in scientific research articles.* Amsterdam: John Benjamins.

———. (1998b). Boosting, hedging and the negotiation of academic knowledge. *TEXT 18*(3), 349–382.

Hyland, K., & Milton, J. (1997). Hedging in L1 and L2 student writing. *Journal of Second Language Writing, 6*(2), 183–206.

Hyland, K., & Tse, P. (2005). *Evaluative that* constructions: Signaling stance in research abstracts. *Functions of Language, 12*(1), 39–64.

Holmes, J. (1988). Doubt and certainty in ESL textbooks. *Applied Linguistics, 9*(1), 20–44.

Lindsay, D. (1984). *A guide to scientific writing.* Melbourne: Longman.

Myers, G. (1992). Textbooks and the sociology of scientific knowledge. *English for Specific Purposes, 11*(1), 3–17.

Strunk, W. J., & White, E. (2000). *The elements of style* (5th ed). New York: Macmillan.

Students Must Learn to Correct All Their Writing Errors

Dana Ferris
California State University–Sacramento

In the Real World

IN 1985, I WAS A 24-YEAR-OLD TEACHING ASSISTANT with a B.A. in literature and creative writing, completing an M.A. in TESOL and teaching my first "real" class of ESL student writers. Though these students had matriculated at a California university, they were at the bottom of four levels of writing instruction, a full three semesters below the college composition level. By several different sets of proficiency indicators, they would have been classified as "low-intermediate" at best.

I worked hard at teaching them grammar—verb tenses, sentence structure, articles, and so forth. I labored over classroom presentations, practice exercises, and tests. I remember struggling nearly the entire semester with trying to get most of the students to write narratives in the simple past tense and to understand that singular count nouns require an article of some sort. At times I thought I was successful—students appeared to understand my explanations and did well on the tests—but then I would receive their next set of papers, and it was as if I had taught them nothing at all!

I took a powerful lesson away from that first experience, one that has shaped my subsequent teaching of ESL composition, my teacher training, my research, and my writing: It is simply not possible to get a whole class of student writers from Point A (wherever they start out) to Point B (perfect, error-free papers) by the end of one writing course. It may not even be possible to get *one* student writer all the way to that elusive Point B. This insight has led me to teach and think and write extensively on realistic and effective ways to "treat" error in student writing (e.g., Ferris, 1995, 1997, 1999, 2002, 2004), focusing particularly on teaching students to self-edit for their most frequent and serious error patterns.

At the same time, I have become increasingly aware of the standards and expectations of the outside world with regard to writing in general and L2 writers in particular. In California, at the time that I wrote this chapter, great controversy swirled about the implementation of the California High School Exit Examination (CAHSEE), which was enforced for the first time for the class of 2006. Some 41,000 seniors failed repeated attempts at this examination, so despite having passed their required classes and completed all other requirements, they were not allowed to graduate with their classmates. In the news stories, the students being "left behind" who were quoted and described had depressingly similar profiles. They were fairly recent immigrants (five years or fewer in the United States) from non–English speaking countries, and they had passed the math portion of the CAHSEE but not the English portion. Similarly, at the California State University, where I teach, there is a system-wide graduation writing requirement. Again, students can pass all of their courses and otherwise be in good standing but be denied their degrees if they fail to pass the writing assessment.

While we ESL writing teachers might believe such writing requirements are inappropriate for English learners or multilingual writers, the fact remains that such hurdles do exist, and not only in California. Thus, while we language professionals may rest in our enlightened awareness that language acquisition takes time, and that progress and not perfection should be our objective, the realities and expectations of the world outside our classrooms often pressure us to reach that unattainable goal. Instead, we must think creatively and strategically about ways to help their students negotiate the gap between what is expected of them and what they may in fact be capable of.

What the Research Says and Shows

Some teachers persist in the belief that if they just work hard enough teaching grammar, correcting written errors, and cracking the whip on the students, they can get students to "correct all their writing errors." As a result, they spend too much time and energy on these matters, frustrating themselves and causing stress for students. However, several interacting strands of research provide strong counterevidence to this belief (really a hope or a wish or a pipe dream). Such studies demonstrate at least three "real-world" truths.

1. **Second language acquisition takes time.**
   Politicians and voters would like to ignore or deny this reality. For example, in 1998 California's Proposition 227 banished bilingual education and allowed children only one year of "structured English immersion" before mainstreaming them. Yet second language acquisition research is quite clear and compelling: It takes years to acquire competence in a second language approaching that of native speakers. When the standard of "competence" is academic literacy tasks required in higher education, the timeline is even longer.

   What this "time" observation means in microcosm is that teachers and students are unlikely to succeed in compressing the SLA process into a fifteen-week course or a single-year immersion program, no matter how hard they try. Rather than envisioning ourselves and our courses as the final stop, we need to perceive ourselves as part of a process that takes years. To restate the lesson learned from my opening anecdote, perhaps "perfect, error-free papers" is Point Z, not Point B, and teachers need to humbly recognize that if students under their care move from Point A to Point C, or Point E to Point H, and so forth, they have been faithful in their responsibilities as links in a much longer chain.

2. **Most L2 writers' texts are observably different from those of native English speakers.**

Studies of English L2 writing have yielded a number of specific findings about the characteristics of L2 texts (Hinkel, 2002; Silva, 1993), or at least those composed by student writers in postsecondary classrooms: Second language writing does not show as much lexical and syntactic variety as texts written by native speakers, and, if the L2 students are educated and literate in other languages, their writing may also be "accented" by contrasting rhetorical patterns. What this means in practice is that even L2 texts that are "error-free" may appear less sophisticated or less idiomatic when compared with native English writers and may be easily identified by readers as being non-native.

While numerous explanations exist for these observable and empirically validated differences, the Occam's Razor version is that L2 writers have not had the equivalent exposure to the patterns of English and especially to English text—from hearing children's stories to reading college textbooks—that builds linguistic competence and provides a range of lexical, syntactic, and rhetorical tools at writers' disposal as they work (Krashen, 2004). Together with the previous observation that SLA takes time, teachers should be reminded that a few grammar lessons are not going to quickly bridge that linguistic schemata gap. When L2 writers make errors, teachers must recognize that such errors do not simply represent a lack of proofreading or a minor short-circuit that can be fixed with a brief rule reminder, but rather that such errors are often clues about what students do not know about the language system as a whole and about written texts in particular.

3. **Even teachers' and students' best efforts at error correction do not result in 100 percent accuracy.**

The question of whether teacher error correction and student editing is effective has sparked much discussion over the past decade. In response to some published debates on the topic, researchers over the past few years have completed studies looking at the short- and long-term effects of teacher intervention with regard to students' written errors. Such studies have delivered good news for teachers who intuitively feel that error correction is needed, that it helps students, and that students want it. When error feedback is thoughtfully and consistently delivered, it can help students to improve the accuracy of their current texts (i.e., in revision); some (limited) evidence further demonstrates that effective error feedback helps students improve in written accuracy over time.

However, even studies delivering "good news" do not find that students produce error-free texts in response to teacher intervention. For instance, in one large semester-long study (Ferris, 2006), students were able to successfully self-edit—at home during revision—approximately 82 percent of the errors called to their attention (but not corrected) by their teachers. In another controlled experimental study (Ferris & Roberts, 2001), students receiving indirect error feedback (i.e., errors were highlighted but not corrected) in five different error categories were able to self-correct, on the spot, 56 percent of their errors. Now, 80 percent success at home and 56 percent in class are pretty good correction ratios, and they definitely provide counterevidence to the argument raised by Truscott (1996, 1999) that students do not pay attention to their teachers' corrections or are unable to utilize the feedback successfully when they do attend to it. Yet these student texts were still not "perfect," not "error-free." Most teachers would agree that no error correction method will ever be effective enough to reach the 100 percent standard. Language is simply too complex, too messy, and the editing process has too many interacting individual variables for any method or approach to be universally successful in helping student writers to achieve perfection. Figure 5.1 summarizes the research in this section.

FIGURE 5.1. Summary of Research

Observation	Some Key Citations
1. Second language acquisition takes time.	Collier (1987, 1989); Doughty & Long (2003); Snow & Hoefnagle-Hohle (1978)
2. Second language writers' texts are different from those written by native English speakers.	Connor (1996, 2003) Hinkel (2002, 2004), Kaplan (1966); Silva (1993)
3. Even diligent teacher correction and student editing does not lead to perfect, error-free texts.	Ferris (2006); Ferris & Roberts (2001); Truscott (1996, 1999)

In sum, while teachers and their students would like to believe that perfection is possible with the right combination of instruction, care, and effort, that is the real myth. It is not, in fact, attainable, at least not in the span of one L2 writing class. Yet, as discussed, not only do teachers and students expect writing to be virtually error-free, but many real-world evaluators outside the individual writing classroom hold that expectation as well.

What We Can Do

So what are teachers to do to help their students bridge that gap between what is *possible,* and what is *expected* (or demanded) of them? To help students realize that they must take seriously real-world demands for written accuracy and to provide them with tools and strategies they will need, L2 writing teachers must consider several principles and design practices that are consistent with those principles. These principles are outlined in Figure 5.2 and discussed.

FIGURE 5.2. Bridging the Gap: Principles and Practices

1. Give students time to do their best work.

2. Help students understand the importance of taking time to think, write, and revise.

3. Teach self-editing strategies, such as reading papers aloud, finding a proofreader, and looking for specific error types one at a time.

4. Hold students accountable for self-editing.

5. Provide expert feedback that focuses on each student's area of greatest need and calls it to their attention and that moves students toward increasing autonomy in self-editing.

6. Understand the limitations of in-class grammar instruction and prioritize self-editing strategies.

1. **Abandon the notion that students can do their best writing under timed conditions.**

It is questionable whether *anyone* can truly excel in writing under time pressure, but this is especially true for L2 student writers. As a case in point, in my own department, we have a junior-level Writing for Proficiency course for multilingual students that helps them to fulfill the CSU graduation writing requirement (Ferris, 2001). Until recently, as I have described elsewhere, student outcomes in this course were determined by a three-hour timed exit examination held on a Saturday morning near the end of the semester; students did not know the topic until they arrived at the exam. These essays were then group-graded using standard holistic scoring practices. The results were depressing. The failure rate on the exam was close to 50 percent. The papers were awful. The teachers and I would sit and look at each other, wondering what we had been doing for the past fifteen weeks and where we had failed. The students, most of whom were close to graduating and had worked extremely hard all semester, were angry and devastated when told they had to repeat the course.

In fairness to ourselves, we did everything possible to help our students succeed under this system. We gave practice exams and taught time-management and "editing under time pressure" strategies (Ferris, 2001, 2002). We taught them all semester about composing processes, rhetorical options, and argumentation. We gave enlightened feedback about content and grammar alike. Still, the outcome was dismal.

A couple of years ago, in response to encouragement from my mainstream (native speaker) composition counterparts in the department, we transitioned the course to portfolio assessment. Now, rather than writing a "one-shot" essay under time pressure on a topic they are unprepared for, students spend twelve weeks discussing topics and readings with their instructors and classmates and producing multiple drafts of several essays. At the end of Week 12, they submit a portfolio of two essays of their choice, a portfolio letter, and an appendix showing earlier drafts and other process artifacts. These are group-graded by a panel of instructors. Students who do not pass the portfolio assessment at that point have an additional three weeks to further revise and polish their essays and letters, which are read again by the portfolio panel.

Though it has taken us several semesters to refine our grading procedures and portfolio requirements, the results have instantly been dramatic. Our pass rate is now close to 90 percent. More important, the quality of the students' writing as demonstrated in the portfolio is substantially better than what we used to see on the timed exit exam. We can see from the students' portfolio letters, from their final essays, and from the drafts and materials they submit that they really have worked hard and learned a lot about writing—which is, after all, the stated purpose of the course.

As to errors in particular, while the portfolio essays are rarely 100 percent error-free, many are virtually so. The gap between what is expected and what students can in fact accomplish has been narrowed by the portfolio process, the components of which include time, multiple attempts at improving their texts (i.e., drafting and revision), expert feedback, and successful strategy instruction. Further, the students' written texts have been improved by, oddly enough, *higher expectations*. Students and teachers are aware that the accuracy standards for the portfolio essays are much higher than they would be for timed essay exams, so they take the feedback, revision, and editing process more seriously. Errors and problems we would have overlooked under the old system are no longer tolerated. In short, by simultaneously *demanding more* yet giving students better *conditions for success,* teachers give students their best opportunity to produce texts that meet high(er) standards. Whether or not teachers and programs adopt portfolio assessment, every classroom can provide students with the benefits of time by allowing for multiple drafting and revising.

2. **Teach students to take the time to write.**

    In addition to structuring our courses and assignments to allow students time to think, draft, and revise, we can teach our students that *taking time* to write is important. We know that students should not be writing papers at the last minute but composing them over a period of days (or weeks) so that they have the time and distance to reflect on what they have written and notice ways to improve their ideas and expression (language). One way I explain the reasons for starting early and revising often is to tell students a story. A number of years ago, I was teaching an ESL composition class that began at 3 PM, and a paper was due that day. The power went out all over campus at about 2:25 PM, coming back on shortly before my class started. Many of my students came to class empty-handed, explaining that they could not finish or print their papers because the electricity was out in the campus computer labs! I pointed out to them (and to every subsequent writing class since) that if they are still finishing a paper 35 minutes before it is due, they have waited too long and cannot possibly be doing their best work. Students smile sheepishly when I tell them this, and no one has ever argued the truth of this assertion with me.

However, as students are usually young and always human, it can be helpful to structure assignments in order to force them out of procrastination habits. Here are several ways to ensure that students take the necessary time. First, give students time to compose and revise their work by including mini-deadlines in each writing assignment. For example, several days before a completed essay draft is due, require students to bring in as homework (or e-mail to you and/or to their writing group) a preliminary draft of the paper. Give them credit for completing it. Tell them that their next task is to take that rough draft, read it the next day, and make any corrections to errors that they find, either in handwritten or electronic form. Ask them to write a paragraph explaining what they found in their papers and what they learned about leaving time and space for proofreading.

3. **Teach students helpful editing strategies.**

While narrowly focused in-class grammar mini-lessons may be useful, the "real-world" constraints described remind us that students' acquisition of language structures cannot be rushed, and that twenty minutes here and there of grammar lessons in the writing class are unlikely to have a huge impact in the short run. What we can accomplish, however, is to help students do a better job of applying the linguistic knowledge they already do have to their written texts. Following are some practical editing strategies that can be easily taught and immediately utilized by student writers.

Strategy 1: Reading Aloud. When writers read their papers aloud, it helps them notice missing words, unnecessary words, and unidiomatic constructions. While L2 writers may not benefit from this technique as much as would a native speaker with stronger intuitions about what "sounds right," they can still pick up a fair amount from this exercise. Though this may be a cumbersome activity if student papers are long, in most instances it will be worth the time spent. You can also suggest that they try reading the paper aloud "backward" (i.e., starting with the final sentence) as a way to see their text differently and attend to word- and sentence-level issues.

> *Sample Exercise.* Ask students to complete an essay draft and print it out. Tell them to read the paper aloud and highlight or mark with a red pen any errors they notice. Ask them to submit their marked paper with a paragraph summarizing what types of errors they found and what they have learned about the benefits of this technique.

Strategy 2: Adding Another Pair of Eyes. I always hesitate briefly before giving this advice, as it almost feels like giving a license to cheat. Every writing teacher has stories of students whose in-class work is full of errors, but whose out-of-class assignments are beautifully edited, leading them to suspect that the student's brother or friend has done the work. Anyone who has ever tutored in a writing center can tell stories of student writers who simply want the tutor to fix their errors rather than teaching them anything about reviewing their own work.

Yet if we as teachers see part of our job as helping students learn how to bridge the gap between expectations and ability, one important life skill is learning to ask others to help us edit our work. Newspapers and publishers employ proofreaders. Many experienced writers rely on writers' groups, more informal types of peer feedback, or, in business settings, administrative assistants. Thus, we should encourage students to find an extra pair of eyes—a tutor, a friend, a classmate—not only to help them pick up what their own proofreading strategies might have missed, but also to help fill in the linguistic gaps they may have as L2 writers. We should remind students to use their own strategies and not to over-rely on others because proofreaders may also miss things and because there will be times when they have to operate independently. Some rules[1] to help them

---

[1] I am grateful to Joy Reid for sharing these tips/rules. The reason behind the penultimate tip is that most native English speakers are likely to do a poor job of explaining grammar rules on the fly.

understand the line between a proofreader (who points things out) and a copy editor (who actually changes things) include:

- The writer must participate actively in the proofing process.
- The proofreader must not use any writing instrument.
- Any changes must be made only by the writer.
- The writer must not ask the proofreader to state a rule.
- The writer should at some point thank or reward the proofreader for his or her help.

Sample Exercises

a. Show the class a sample text or excerpt written by a student at the same level of instruction. Give them time to read through the text and mark any errors that they notice. Debrief what they have found in pairs or in groups and as a whole class with a teacher-marked version. Then have students exchange papers they are working on with a classmate, asking the classmate to point out but not correct any problems they see. The partners should have time to discuss each other's findings and have opportunity to ask the teacher if they are confused or in disagreement about a point. This low-stakes exercise drives home the point that it can be easier to find errors in another writer's work than in one's own (Ferris, 1995).

b. Ask students to take a preliminary draft of a paper they are working on to a campus writing center or other tutor (anyone more expert than they are in English and in writing). Ask them to take notes on their papers about what they discussed and what they learned from the tutoring session and to write a paragraph for you describing and/or evaluating the experience.

c. Hand out a student sample with numerous errors, giving students ten minutes to proof and correct every error they find. Then ask the entire class to stand up. Ask, "How many of you found and corrected five or fewer errors?" Tell those who raise their hands to sit down. "How many found 10 or fewer errors?" They sit down. Depending on how many errors are present, the last question is "How many found X errors or more?" As those students remain standing, tell the class, "These are the students you want proofing your papers!"[2]

Strategy 3: Making Separate Passes Through a Text for Different Error Patterns. As noted in Ferris (2002), certain error types are fairly pervasive in English L2 writing, and some error types are more "treatable" (Ferris, 1999), meaning they are at least somewhat governed by rules that can be explained and applied. Examples of "treatable" errors include most verb-related categories (tense, form, passives, modal use, etc.), while "untreatable" errors might include word choice (such as prepositions) and unidiomatic phrase or sentence structure. One helpful editing strategy is to teach students to make separate passes through their texts to look specifically for "treatable" structures/errors one at a time. Many students have found that the advice to look only at verb phrases or only at noun endings can be much more helpful than simply, "Read through your paper and correct any errors you might find." Reading their papers and looking only for one error type can be especially empowering if the teacher has already identified specific types of errors as problematic for that particular student writer as she or he learns skills to make progress on those errors.

Sample Exercise. Give students a text excerpt that contains a number of easily recognizable errors in a "treatable" category, like plural endings on nouns. Using highlighters, ask them to go through the text, marking every noun phrase. Then have them circle nouns that could potentially take plural endings (i.e., countable). Finally, have them underline every circled noun that has a plural error (missing, unnecessary, erroneous form). Discuss findings as a whole

---

[2] This exercise was shared by Joy Reid.

class and answer any questions. Ask students to repeat the exercise with a partner's paper or with their own papers.

4. **Hold students accountable for applying editing strategies.**
One of the reasons our portfolio course has been so successful is that both teachers and students understand that the grading standards and expectations are higher than under the previous exit examination model. Besides teaching the editing strategies and giving students exercises and assignments to help them practice the tools, teachers then should be diligent in holding students accountable for submitting well-edited papers, at least after several drafts through the process. One way to both reinforce the editing strategies and to encourage students to use them is to ask students to write a brief reflection on which of the editing strategies they used and found most helpful. A more ambitious approach would be to have students highlight subsequent drafts of papers, showing errors they found in an earlier draft and corrected in a later draft.

I also make it clear to my students that papers that have not been spell-checked will be returned to them unread and ungraded. I should not spend my time circling typos when students should be responsible for taking the two minutes needed to run a spell-check. I make sure that they know how to use spell-check and that they understand its limits (Ferris & Hedgcock, 2005). If students are not systematically running spell-check on all their papers for school, they should be, and they should make it a lifelong habit. I point out this goes for email, too, when the correspondence is of a formal nature, and show them on a couple of different email editors where the spell-check is located.

Sample Exercise. Have students complete an essay draft and print it out. If they have spell-check turned on as they type, ask them to mark with a red pen or a highlighter every word the spell-check marks before making corrections. Or, if they turn off spelling and grammar checking as they type, have them run the spell-check on the entire document, again marking spelling or typing errors found. These exercises will help them to notice how many spelling or typing errors they make and how important it is to use the spell-check feature every time they are writing something for others to read.

5. **Be diligent, consistent, and systematic in providing error feedback that can help student writers to make progress in accuracy.**

Teacher feedback on student errors needs to do far more than simply point out what is wrong in a particular paper. Rather, it should (a) help students know from the beginning of the course what their specific trouble spots are; (b) help raise student awareness of specific language issues through in-text, point-of-error feedback; and (c) move students toward increasing autonomy in finding and correcting their own language problems. Specific suggestions for each goal are outlined.

Feedback Strategy A: Identify Individual Error Patterns.
Depending on the linguistic/cultural makeup and the English proficiency level of a particular group of students, different students may have varying language problems. In my own rather heterogeneous classes, I often will have a "word order" group, a "verb tense" group, and an "articles" group—with no overlap among them. As a result, I have found that completing an individualized error analysis for each student is very helpful for them and for me in charting the course for individual feedback as well as class and small group mini-lessons during the semester. I have described my procedures for doing this elsewhere (Ferris, 2002), but I have since stumbled upon a more streamlined way of accomplishing this rather arduous task.

Sample Exercise. Have students complete a short piece of writing either in class or out of class. Then, highlight error-specific error categories. Between three and seven categories is probably optimal. Next, review the categories with the students. Then have them number each error you have marked consecutively and log the error into the appropriate category on an error chart. They can ask peers or the teacher for help. Finally, ask them to total their errors in the various categories and list top three problem areas on a summary form. (Sample workshop materials are provided in the appendix to this chapter.) Spot-check the papers and charts for accurate categorization.[3] Collect the individual forms and compile a class summary form to show the students later. Then you and the students will both know what areas of need individuals have and what problems are somewhat common to the whole class.

Feedback Strategy B: Identify and Mark Errors in Student Papers.

I have written extensively elsewhere about issues and options with regard to expert feedback on student errors (e.g., Ferris, 2002, 2003; Ferris & Hedgcock, 2005). Below I describe briefly some techniques and procedures for helping students understand and make progress in their most frequent and serious patterns through teacher feedback on their papers.

Step 1: On early drafts of papers, take note of the most major error problems, ideally no more than two or three patterns at once. Along with other issues of content and organization, in a summary note to the writer, identify the patterns (e.g., "Be sure to check your nouns to see if they need a plural ending."). Then highlight instances of errors in those specific categories in the draft. You may wish to

---

[3] Generally speaking, with only a few clearly defined categories, with the errors already highlighted for them, and with time to chart and ask questions, I have found that my students do pretty well on the task. The entire activity takes me 2–3 hours, and the in-class activity can be accomplished in 30 minutes or so.

highlight all of them or just a portion (a page or a couple of paragraphs, depending on the length of the paper). You may or may not wish to add error codes *(pl)* or rule reminders *(past tense)* to the highlighted errors.

Step 2: On a later or penultimate draft, mark (highlight, with or without codes) all instances of errors throughout the paper in the major categories you have identified for that student/paper.

Step 3: On the final draft before a portfolio submission or grade, respond by marking remaining errors of any type. At this point, if there are "untreatable" errors (lexical errors in particular, such as prepositions), you might wish to provide the correct form for the student's information.

> *Sample Exercise.* Using a predefined set of error categories, ask students to chart the number of errors marked in each category in an error log or error chart, and have them maintain that chart throughout the semester. Students can chart the number of errors for each paper (or drafts of different papers) marked in each category, noting their progress from draft to draft and hopefully from paper to paper. An excerpt of such an error log is provided in Table 5.1. Note that the three error types would have been identified during Step 1 (above). Also, it is not surprising to see that, as the word count increases through revisions and over time, there are actually more errors in some categories. Error frequencies should be considered as ratios (to number of words) rather than simple raw numbers. (See Ferris & Roberts, 2001, for a description of how these can be calculated.)

Feedback Strategy C: Encourage Student Autonomy.
I return here to the principle of student accountability. If the ultimate goal of treating student error is to help them bridge the gap between the expectation of "virtually error-free

TABLE 5.1. Excerpt: Student Error Log

Student Name: <u>Nozomi</u>

Most Frequent/Serious Errors: <u>articles, plural endings, prepositions</u>

Paper/Draft #	# of Words	Article Errors	Plural Ending Errors	Preposition Errors
Essay 1, Draft A	425	9	5	3
Essay 1, Draft B	510	4	3	3
Essay 1, Draft C	565	1	0	1
Essay 2, Draft A	520	7	6	4
Essay 2, Draft B	620	5	2	4
Essay 2, Draft C	715	2	0	2
Continue for later assignments and final revisions.				

papers" that many readers outside the L2 composition class hold and their still-developing linguistic competence, then systematically and intentionally moving students toward greater autonomy in finding and editing their own work is a critical step. Teachers can build autonomy in several ways. First, in giving feedback, the teacher might want to move from more explicit (all errors marked in the text with codes or labels) to less so (no labels, fewer errors marked, verbal summary notes but no in-text markings) as the course goes along.

Second, as students are taught and then practice a range of editing strategies, teachers can ask them to do more and more of their own self-editing—and teachers can mark fewer and fewer drafts of papers. Teachers should remind students that diligence and attention to errors is expected and will be considered in their final assessment. Table 5.2 gives another version of a Student Error Chart, which can be used with Feedback Strategy C.

TABLE 5.2. Student Error Chart

Error #	Noun Ending	Verb	Article	Word Choice	Sentence Structure	Mechanics	Other
1							
2							
3							
4							
5							
6							
7							
8							
9							
10							
TOTALS							

6. **Recognize that in-class grammar instruction has a limited role in solving students' error problems.**

   Writing teachers tend to focus almost obsessively on finding the right lessons, practice exercises, websites, and so forth in the attempt to find the magic bullet that will get students to that elusive Point B (or Z). But as my first class over twenty years ago taught me, even the best taught grammar lessons do not automatically translate into improved texts. Given the realities that our time with students is short and that we cannot fast-forward the time that second language development takes, our time is much better spent (a) teaching students solid self-editing strategies that they can use for many years to come and (b) providing text-specific error feedback to each individual student in their areas of greatest need. While some brief, narrowly focused instruction on treatable error patterns that is explicitly connected to other editing instruction may be valuable (Ferris, 2002; Ferris & Hedgcock, 2005; Frodesen & Holten, 2003), it is critically important that any such instruction include immediate and directed application to the students' own writing.

L2 writing teachers and their students have a problem. Actually, they have two problems. One is that the world outside of their writing classes may be far less forgiving and understanding of L2 writers' written errors, linguistic gaps, and acquisition processes. The other problem is that the teachers and students themselves persist in the belief that if they just work hard enough, students will produce error-free papers at the end of a course. As I said earlier, this is the real myth—not whether students must learn to correct all their errors, but whether they *can*. However, with the right combination of time, strategy training, feedback, and accountability, students may leave their writing class with lifelong skills that will help them to bridge the gaps they will face between what is expected of them and what they are capable of doing. If teachers will invest the thought, time, and energy it will take to equip students with those skills, it will be a great gift to them.

Questions for Reflection

1. Is it your belief, observation, or experience that high standards of written accuracy are expected in academic or professional settings? If you disagree, why? If you agree, how does that awareness affect your teaching practices?

2. This chapter argues that structuring a writing course/assessment so that students have adequate time and space to reflect upon and self-edit their writing is a critical step toward helping students learn to produce writing that meets high standards. Is this consistent with your own beliefs and practices? If so, how do you practice this belief in your writing classroom?

3. One objection that could be raised to the "time" principle is that students will plagiarize or cheat if they are not required to do their writing under timed, secure conditions. Is this a compelling argument? If so, are there ways to mitigate this potential problem and still allow students adequate revising and editing time in the course?

4. This chapter argues that systematically training students in self-editing strategies and holding them accountable for utilizing these skills is far more valuable and productive than in-class grammar instruction for helping students to learn to correct their written errors. What are the arguments presented throughout this chapter that lead to this claim, and what is your opinion of those arguments? How are they similar to or different from your own teaching practices, and would you now change any of your practices?

5. What are some new skills or ideas presented in this chapter that you would like to try?

References

Collier, V. P. (1987). Age and rate of acquisition of second language for academic purposes. *TESOL Quarterly, 21*, 617–641.

——. (1989). How long? A synthesis of research on academic achievement in a second language. *TESOL Quarterly, 23*, 509–531.

Connor, U. (1996). *Contrastive rhetoric cross-cultural aspects of second-language writing.* New York: Cambridge University Press.

——. (2003). Changing currents in contrastive rhetoric: Implications for teaching and research. In B. Kroll (Ed.), *Exploring the dynamics of second language writing* (pp. 218–241). Cambridge, UK: Cambridge University Press.

Doughty, C., & Long, M. H. (2003). *The handbook of second language acquisition.* Malden, MA: Blackwell.

Ferris, D. R. (1995). Teaching ESL composition students to become independent self-editors. *TESOL Journal, 4(4)*, 18–22.

——. (1997). The influence of teacher commentary on student revision. *TESOL Quarterly, 31*, 315–339.

——. (1999). The case for grammar correction in L2 writing classes: A response to Truscott (1996). *Journal of Second Language Writing, 8,* 1–10.

——. (2001). Teaching writing proficiency in summer school: Lessons from a foxhole. In J. Murphy & P. Byrd (Eds.), *Understanding the courses we teach: Local perspectives on English language teaching.* (pp. 328–345). Ann Arbor: University of Michigan Press.

——. (2002). *Treatment of error in second language student writing.* Ann Arbor: University of Michigan Press.

——. (2003). *Response to student writing: Implications for second language students.* Mahwah, NJ: Lawrence Erlbaum.

——. The "grammar correction" debate in L2 writing: Where are we, and where do we go from here? *Journal of Second Language Writing, 13,* 1–14.

——. (2006). Does error feedback help student writers? New evidence on the short- and long-term effects of written error correction. In K. Hyland & F. Hyland (Eds.), *Feedback in second language writing: Contexts and issues.* (pp. 81–104). Cambridge, UK: Cambridge University Press.

Ferris, D. R., & Hedgcock, J. S. (2005). *Teaching ESL composition: Purpose, process, & practice* (2nd ed.). Mahwah, NJ: Lawrence Erlbaum.

Ferris, D., & Roberts, B. (2001). Error feedback in L2 writing classes: How explicit does it need to be? *Journal of Second Language Writing, 10,* 161–184.

Frodesen, J., & Holten, C. (2003). Grammar and the ESL writing class. In B. Kroll (Ed.), *Exploring the dynamics of second language writing* (pp. 141–161). Cambridge, UK: Cambridge University Press.

Hinkel, E. (2002). *Second language writers' text: Linguistic and rhetorical features.* Mahwah, NJ: Lawrence Erlbaum.

Hinkel, E. (2004). *Teaching academic ESL writing: Practical techniques in vocabulary and grammar.* Mahwah, NJ: Lawrence Erlbaum.

Kaplan, R. B. (1966). Cultural thought patterns in intercultural communication. *Language Learning, 16,* 1–20.

Krashen, S. D. (2004). *The power of reading* (2nd ed.). Westport, CT: Libraries Unlimited.

Silva, T. (1993). Toward an understanding of the distinct nature of L2 writing: The ESL research and its implications. *TESOL Quarterly, 27,* 657–677.

Snow, C., & Hoefnagle-Hohle, M. (1978). The critical period for language acquisition: Evidence from second language learning. *Child Development, 49,* 1114–1128.

Truscott, J. (1996). The case against grammar correction in L2 writing classes. *Language Learning, 46,* 327–369.

Truscott, J. (1999). The case for "the case for grammar correction in L2 writing classes": A response to Ferris. *Journal of Second Language Writing, 8,* 111–122.

Appendix

Sample Materials for In-Class Diagnostic Error Analysis ——

Diagnostic Essay Editing Workshop

1. **Individually:** Go through the highlighted marks on your essay and number them in order. Then try to classify each error into an error category. Complete the attached chart. If you are confused about an error category, put a question mark (?) in the chart for now.

2. **In groups of 3:** Go over your charts together. See if anyone in your group can help you with any question marks in your chart. Also see if anyone can suggest a correction if you can't think of one.

3. **Individually:** Complete the Error Analysis Summary Form and give it to me when you are finished.

Error Categories

Verb Error: The verb is in the wrong tense or has the wrong form or does not agree in number with the subject.

Noun Ending Error: The noun has a missing plural or possessive ending, the wrong ending, or an unnecessary ending.

Article Error: There is a missing, wrong, or unnecessary article.

Word Choice Error: The wrong word or word form is used.

Sentence Structure Error: The sentence has missing or extra words, the wrong word order, or is a sentence fragment or run-on sentence.

Mechanics: Other errors in spelling, punctuation, or capitalization.

Examples

1. verb   I didn't buy the car because I **didn't wanted** to spend so much money.

2. noun ending   We all rushed to help because my **uncles** house was on fire.

3. verb   I didn't worry about my English. Now, I **understood** how important it is.

4. word choice   I looked at all of the cars and picked **up** the one I wanted.

5. sentence structure For immigrants **there always something** that makes them live unhappily in this country.

6. article   When you are **student**, you always have to study hard.

Error Analysis Summary Form

Error Type	Number of Errors You Found
Verbs	
Noun Endings	
Articles	
Word Choice	
Sentence Structure	
Mechanics	
Totals	

What are your three most important error categories to work on during this class?

1. _____

2. _____

3. _____

Do you have any comments or questions about errors you would like to work on during this course?

1. _____

2. _____

3. _____

MYTH

Corpus-Based Research Is Too Complicated to Be Useful for Writing Teachers

Susan Conrad
Portland State University

In the Real World

THE APPLAUSE AT THE END OF MY TALK had barely quieted down when the woman from the third row approached me. I had been speaking to faculty in a university English department in the southern United States, and I had noticed this woman even before I began the talk. She had settled into a seat in the front of the room and flipped through my handout—a handout full of numbers, statistics, and figures. A look somewhere between confusion and horror had settled on her face. "Oh no," I thought, "this is going to be a disaster."

I was speaking about a research study that used a corpus linguistics approach. This approach involves using computers to analyze large collections of transcribed spoken or written texts. The strength of using a large corpus is that we can see what language choices typically occur in certain contexts when we consider many different writers (or speakers).

Concerning academic writing, for example, I have heard some teachers claim that first person pronouns *(I, we)* are not appropriate in the sciences and passive voice should be used, and they have many selected examples to prove their point. However, corpus-based study can show us that scientific articles do sometimes use first person pronouns, and that in many cases, rather than using passive voice, articles have active voice verbs with inanimate subjects (such as, *the results indicate . . .*). To find the patterns over many texts, corpus linguists use quantitative analysis—such as counts or statistics comparing the frequencies of different grammatical structures or different words. The language choices are then described fully by looking at how the grammar and vocabulary are used in the texts. The ultimate goal—describing how language is used—is helpful for any language teacher, but I knew many people who had a block against numbers and statistics. After all, they'd gone into language because they hated math! They took one look at corpus studies and saw numbers, tables, figures, statistics, computers, and they decided corpus linguistics was too foreign, too mathematical, just too **complicated** for them.

The specific study I was presenting showed how language varies across different types of academic writing. For example, it compared textbooks and research articles and it compared students' papers in university history and biology courses (two common choices for fulfilling general education requirements in U.S. universities). The study was clearly applicable to faculty in this English department, which offered writing courses for all students at the university. But with many faculty trained in literature, creative writing, and rhetoric, I had suspected this audience was likely to be a tough one, and that look of confusion and horror over my handout convinced me I was right.

The woman from the third row made it to the podium, and I winced inwardly, reminding myself to be sympathetic. Then a big smile broke out on her face. "I just have to tell you—I understood this! I looked at this handout at the beginning and saw all those numbers and charts and thought, 'There is no way I can make sense of this,' but you explained it and I understood! I can understand this! And it's really interesting!"

Since that talk in early 1996, I have seen a lot of people, including my own undergraduate students, take a first look at corpus-based research and think there was no way they could understand it. But almost all those who have spent a few minutes reading a study or listening to an explanation have discovered that they *can* understand the work and that they learn things about texts that they could not have learned any other way. Despite the myth that corpus linguistics is weird, complicated, esoteric work, it is in fact a useful approach to learning about language, and it is directly applicable to teaching writing.

What the Research Says and Shows

Corpus-based research can focus on virtually any type of writing. Because I have most often taught (and studied) writing for academic purposes in an American university context, that is what I focus on here. Specifically, I review the three findings that have been the most important to me personally as a teacher of academic writing (summarized in Figure 6.1). Keep in mind, though, that if you teach other types of writing, other corpus-based research will be more useful for your context.

FIGURE 6.1. What the Research Says

Observations	Some Key Corpus-Based Publications
1. The language needed to argue or persuade in academic writing is very different from the language used in everyday arguments, such as in newspaper editorials or conversations.	Biber (1988); Biber, Johansson, Leech, Conrad, & Finegan (1999); Biber, Conrad, Reppen, Byrd, & Helt (2002)
2. In any discipline, the patterns of language features reflect not only the subject area, but the methods for building knowledge.	Conrad (1996); Conrad (2001); Stoller, Jones, Costanza-Robinson, & Robinson (2005)
3. Formulaic language chunks (also called lexical bundles) are very useful in academic writing.	Biber, Conrad & Cortes (2004); Biber, Johansson, Leech, Conrad, & Finegan (1999); Cortes (2004); Granger (1998)

<u>Observation 1</u>: **The language needed to argue or persuade in academic writing is very different from the language used in everyday arguments, such as in newspaper editorials or conversations.**

When ESL textbooks ask students to *write to persuade,* they often raise controversial social issues, such as designating English as an official language or the benefits of working mothers versus stay-at-home mothers. For many teachers, the common meaning of *argument* raises the image of issues like these that have opposing sides, with each trying to persuade the other of the correct perspective. These are the kinds of issues that we hear debates about or read in newspaper editorials—stating a particular point of view on an issue and explaining why a previous point of view was wrong or what actions should be taken. In real academic writing, however—as opposed to the practice that EAP students are often given—an *argument* and a writer's means of persuading take a very different form. Rarely is there an issue with clear opposing sides. Instead, a claim about new knowledge is made. This might be an analysis of the writer's own data (as in a research article) or an interpretation of other sources (as in literature reviews and textbooks). Writers persuade their readers by analyzing their data or sources in a principled way and leading readers through their interpretations and conclusions.

Because arguing and persuading are so different in academic writing than in typical everyday arguments, the language features that are most typical are also very different. Corpus-based research such as that listed in Section 1 of Figure 6.1 is especially useful for ESL teachers because it highlights the difference in language between everyday arguments and academic arguments. For example, newspaper editorials—which often deal with controversial social issues—typically have language features that very overtly mark persuasion: certain modal verbs such as *will, would,* and *should* (e.g., *it would be a mistake to . . . , you should really . . .*) and conditional clauses that refer to future events and options in a situation (*if we are to . . .*). Similarly, conversations often have opinions marked in very explicit ways with first person pronouns and particular verbs (e.g., *I think, I know*). These language features of "everyday" arguments are listed in Figure 6.2.

FIGURE 6.2. Language Features that Show Overt Argument and Persuasion*

modal verbs that express prediction and suggestion (e.g. *would, should*)	*It **would** be a mistake to . . .* *You **should** really . . .*
conditional clauses that refer to predicted future events or options	***If** we are to . . .*
first-person pronoun + verb showing thought or belief used to express ideas	***I think** . . .* ***I believe** there must be . . .*
expressions that overtly identify an opinion	***In my opinion** . . .* *Well, **my opinion** is . . .*
first-person pronoun + verb showing suggestion or agreement	***suggest** that you . . .* ***I recommend** this one . . .* ***I agree** with you.*

In contrast to newspaper editorials and conversation, academic writing only rarely uses overt features of persuasion and personal judgment. Consider this article in American history about peddlers in the late eighteenth and early nineteenth centuries:

> Peddlers brought to the rural peoples of the northern United States a new culture, a market culture, in the form of objects. Peddlers helped create a market for new consumer goods: chairs, clocks, books, and portraits. Their commercial activities weakened the structure of local exchange. . . .
>
> (Jaffee, 1991, p. 511)

The passage has none of the features of overt persuasion. It reads like statements of fact, using simple past tense verbs. It turns out, however, that these statements are the main argument of the article, and the author spends the next twenty pages supporting these ideas—describing the rural economies before the peddlers, discussing the peddlers' activities, and illustrating how household goods and consumers' habits changed after the peddlers came through.

One result that corpus-based analysis demonstrates is that in a research paper the statement of the main claim—the actual argument—does not look like a claim at all. It typically uses simple present or

---

* These features are relatively rare in academic writing.

simple past tense verbs. Similarly, opinions and recommendations are usually stated without verbs that explicitly mark opinion:

> Learners require opportunities for both form-focused and function-focused practice in the development of particular skill areas. . . .
>
> (from the *Longman Spoken and Written English Corpus;*
> see Biber et al., 1999, Chapter 1)

However, ESL students (and novice native-speaker writers too) often expect overtly persuasive language even in academic texts. As a consequence, in reading academic texts, they often miss the fact that there is any attempt at persuasion because they do not see the overtly persuasive features that they are used to. When writing, they often state their arguments in language more typical of conversation, as in these advanced-level ESL student paper excerpts:

> *In my opinion* their lack of understanding is related to their different backgrounds and dissimilar perception of the events. . . .
>
> *I think* that they succeeded in the sustainable development with a syncretic culture of their tradition and modern technology.
>
> (from The Viking Corpus of Student
> Academic Writing; see Albers, 2007)

Many students also use the modals and conditionals more typical of newspaper editorials when they emphasize a point or structure their ideas in academic papers:

> That is the reason why *we should be aware* of these issues.
>
> I can't help thinking *they should have learned* the language more before arriving. . . .
>
> Sustainability is possible *if we recognize that* we are a part of the ecosystem.
>
> (from The Viking Corpus of Student
> Academic Writing; see Albers, 2007)

Proficient academic writing is a form of persuasive language and it does give individuals' perspectives, but the types of arguments and the language forms that are used are different from the overtly persuasive kinds of language that most ESL students learn.

<u>Observation 2</u>: **In any discipline, the patterns of language features reflect not only the subject area, but the methods for building knowledge.**

Although most academic writing is similar in having few overt features of argument or persuasion, the language varies from discipline to discipline. This is obvious for vocabulary, but it is also true for grammar. The types of questions that a discipline addresses, the methods that are used to gather and analyze information, and even the type of information that is considered appropriate all affect language choices. The corpus-based research in Section 2 of Figure 6.1 has taught me to look very closely at how different disciplines use language.

One illustration of how language features are used differently across disciplines can be seen by comparing statements of methods and general interpretations in biology versus history. In biology, explanations of specific methods (and results) for a study are in past tense, while the more global statements of interpretation are in present tense. For instance, in a study investigating whether birds limit grasshopper populations, the authors explain:

> <u>Methods</u>: We *established* a 75-m interval grid on the study mesa that *included* 48 grid intersection points (Fig. 1). We then *measured* grasshopper densities from June through mid-October. . . .

> <u>Results</u>: By the final year of the study, mean annual adult grasshopper density *was* >2.2 times higher on plots from which birds *were* excluded . . .

> <u>Generalization from the results</u>: Grasshopper population dynamics *appear* to be affected by many variables. . . . Results of the present field experiment in Arizona . . . *indicate* that avian predation can also limit grasshopper densities in a variety of ecosystems.

> (Bock, Bock, & Grant, 1992, pp. 1707, 1710, 1715)

History has the opposite pattern of present and past tense use. The more global statements about the study's contribution to our understanding of history tend to be in past tense (for example in the above passage, *peddlers brought to the rural people a new culture*). Statements about methods usually concern the evidence that the writer used to reach the interpretations, with justifications given in present tense. For example, one writer explains his procedures for answering the question of whether the Plains Indian tribes had an ecological equilibrium with bison populations in the early 1800s as follows:

> Answering that question *involves* an effort to come to grips with the factors affecting bison populations, the factors affecting Indian populations, and the cultural aspects of Plains' Indians' utilization of bison. Each of the three aspects of the question *presents* puzzles difficult to resolve. . . .
>
> (Flores, 1991, p. 476)

Another writer explains why it is helpful to analyze ads about runaway slaves in order to understand more about slave life:

> To historians, however, runaway ads invariably *stand* as extraordinary documents…they *provide* brisk but arresting portraits of people. . . . The ads thus *inform* us about constituencies.
>
> (Prude, 1991, p. 125–126)

These historians use present tense to argue the continuing justification or importance for their evidence today.

The opposite patterns for past and present verb tense use between biology and history are associated with the different goals and methods of the disciplines. Biology is interested in describing general processes and ongoing behaviors for plants and animals, so the more global interpretations are made in simple present (and appropriately hedged, as will be discussed). In contrast, part of convincing readers that interpretations are justified is a clear accounting of exactly what happened in the particular study—thus, methodological procedures are past tense narratives, and results are in past tense for the particular case. In history, on the other hand, the interpretation focuses on the past and explains why or how something happened. Since the interpretive statements are about the past, they use past tense. Those history studies that discuss their data (and not all do) have to make an argument for why those artifacts or procedures are valuable today—and thus use present tense. (For additional discussion of grammar use in academic disciplines, see the Byrd & Bunting chapter in this volume.)

If you think that undergraduate students at universities do not have to write in disciplinary-specific ways, you may want to think again. The research studies noted in Figure 6.1 found that in both history and biology, even students in second-year courses were asked to do papers that were like original research in that discipline (much shorter and less involved, but written similarly). And even in majors where you might think writing is not very important, faculty are concerned about writing; for example, the Stoller et al. (2005) article in Figure 6.1 discusses writing for chemistry majors. If we want to prepare students for writing for different disciplines, we can't ignore variation in language use, and corpus-based studies provide a way of seeing the patterns across many disciplines.

Observation 3: Formulaic language chunks (also called lexical bundles) are very useful in academic writing.

Another area of corpus-based research that has been very useful to me for teaching writing concerns what is called *formulaic language* or *multi-word units* or lexical bundles. All of these terms are used to mean units of more than two words that occur repeatedly over many texts and many authors. They may be complete phrases (such as *in other words*) or they may be incomplete structures (such as *it may be that*). In either case, they are convenient building blocks for ideas within the texts.

The research listed in Section 3 of Figure 6.1 highlights certain points about these lexical bundles. One is that they are more common in conversation, where we tend to use a smaller range of words and phrases. However, Biber et al. (1999) find that even in academic prose, repeated bundles of three or four words account for about 20 percent of the discourse. That means about one-fifth of the words are in these recurring chunks that multiple authors use, not in new creative language made just for that text. Further, these bundles prove to be useful in a wide variety of texts. For example, here you can see the bundle *it is important to* in four very different subject areas and contexts:

applied linguistics: *It is important to* recognize that the difference involves only a statistical trend, not a categorical distinction.

biology: Having seen how variation can arise, and how populations can change, *it is important to* address the question of how variation can be maintained in natural populations.

psychology: Because dreamers sometimes project unconscious complexes onto persons known to them, *it is important to* help the dreamer distinguish between dream images that are taken subjectively and those taken objectively.

marketing: Given this reality of selective attention, *it is important to* understand what factors influence the consumer's allocation of this limited resource, particularly for those seeking to attract the consumer's attention.

> (from the TOEFL® 2000 Spoken and Written Academic
> Language Corpus, see Biber et al. 2002; and the Corpus of
> Writing in the Academic Disciplines, see Conrad, 2001)

Some of the most interesting bundles in academic writing are useful when authors show their certainty and attitudes—called *stance bundles* in the research because authors are displaying their stance (i.e., their opinions, judgments, and attitudes) toward the information. Sentence stems such as *it is possible that, it is likely that,* and *it may be that* are ways that writers can get in their preferred explanations while hedging appropriately. Bundles such as, *it is important to* and *it is interesting to* tell writers' assessment of significance. Other bundles show that an idea is based on evidence from studies: *have been shown to, was found to be,* and *studies have shown that.* Finally, other bundles name logical relationships that are hard to express without a condensed expression: *as a result of* and *as a function of*. (For a full discussion of hedging, see Myth 4, Hyland, in this volume.)

When I first began teaching writing, I often focused on helping students be creative. I encouraged more diversity in vocabulary and more creative word use. From corpus-based research, I have learned that using the typical language structures for certain meanings is actually a sign of proficiency. Using these bundles is not plagiarism; it is a matter of giving readers expected forms that they read efficiently.

Cortes' (2004) study builds on previous lexical bundle work by showing that, although some chunks are shared across disciplines, there are also different chunks used by different disciplines. She also found in her study that even native speaker students often fail to use the bundles or use them in inappropriate ways. For example, professional writers in history use *at the same time* to mean simultaneously in time—which makes sense given history's subject matter. Students, however, used *at the same time* in a metaphorical sense, to add an idea. Granger's (1998) study found that second language students tend to use just a few formulaic expressions and to use them repeatedly rather than using different bundles effectively for different functions.

Lack of appropriate lexical bundles will rarely stop a reader's comprehension, but it does make students sound less knowledgeable and less academically sophisticated, especially when they are writing for experts in their field (as students have to do). (For additional discussion of vocabulary use in academic writing, see the Folse chapter in this volume.) Furthermore, not using typical bundles often leaves students using other expressions that they are more familiar with, usually from conversation; they use *I think* rather than *it may be that*, or *I want to say that* rather than *it is interesting to note*. The slight change in wording affects the conveyed meaning. *I think* sounds like an individual opinion, while *it may be that* or *it is possible that* conveys one of several alternative explanations.

When I think over what I have learned about academic writing from corpus-based studies, I sometimes feel rather foolish. Shouldn't I have been able to explain all these language patterns to my students before reading and doing corpus-based research? Didn't I really know these things about academic writing already?

In fact, I did "know" some of these things. Having written my way successfully through a lot of academic work, I knew what writing was like in certain academic disciplines. But it was only when I saw the patterns of language that emerge in corpus-based studies that I consciously realized and could explain how language forms were being used. I also had false intuition about some fields; I never expected, for example, to find present tense methodological passages in history writing. This is why corpus-based research is important for writing teachers: Although we "know" a lot, we aren't always conscious of how language is used, and sometimes our intuitions or anecdotal evidence are misleading. It can be as difficult for teachers as for our students to notice typical language choices, especially in complicated texts like academic writing. Corpus-based studies are a way of investigating the patterns in a large number of texts that cover many different authors so that we can see what is typical and what is unusual. To believe the myth that corpus linguistics research is just too complicated to be helpful for teaching writing is to cheat yourself and your students of very useful information.

What We Can Do

Even if you never want to do corpus linguistics work yourself, your teaching can benefit from it. Seven suggestions follow. I start with the single easiest and most important suggestion for teaching any kind of writing. I continue with five applications of the specific academic writing research I reviewed. I then conclude with a suggestion for how to start pursuing your own corpus work in case you are intrigued enough to find out more.

1. **Refer to corpus-based research to learn about the type of language used in whatever kind of writing you teach.**

   Even if you never look at a corpus yourself, it is worth continuing to keep up with corpus-based research. First, if some findings that were briefly mentioned in this chapter interest you, get the whole story; for instance, if you are interested in how students use lexical bundles differently than professionals do, read the Cortes (2004) article. You can get additional information about academic prose and about other kinds of writing through corpus-based research that is now being published and presented at conferences every year. Even if you have thought of research studies as too difficult or boring in the past, try learning about the results of more corpus-based work. When research helps you understand different types of writing, it is fascinating to read.

   If you regularly teach academic writing, a corpus-based reference that specifically addresses differences in features between academic writing and other types of discourse is invaluable and will give you information far beyond what I have covered here. For example, next time you are teaching students about the choice of active versus passive voice in academic writing, you could first refer to the *Longman Grammar of Spoken and Written English* (Biber et al., 1999) to increase your own understanding of passives—seeing, for instance, what role passives usually play in cohesion, under what conditions professional academic writers typically include agent *by*-phrases with their passives, and what verbs are most typically used in passive voice. Corpus-based references are different from other grammar books because they discuss how grammar structures are typically used in different kinds of speech and writing, not just what is grammatical and ungrammatical.

2. **When choosing academic writing textbooks, look for books that have samples of real writing from disciplinary sources— not just popular magazines and not examples written (or highly modified) for the ESL textbook.**

   Another relatively straightforward change to make in teaching concerns the criteria you use to choose a textbook. Most ESL writing texts contain readings or samples of writing. When choosing a book, many teachers pay little attention to where these readings come from, considering instead only the level of vocabulary and whether the topics might be interesting to their students. These are important concerns, of course, but it's equally important to look at the sources of the texts. If they are popular magazines or newspapers, they will not be showing students the type of argumentation or the lexical bundles that are typical for academic writing. Don't confuse different topics with different purposes and audiences, and if you are teaching writing for academic purposes, make sure that your textbook has writing from academic sources such as textbooks and articles from journals. If you must use a textbook that doesn't have academic sources or has passages so heavily "adapted" that they have lost the typical language features of academic prose, supplement the textbook with texts that you gather that exemplify typical academic prose. (And you will know what features are typical from consulting the corpus-based studies and references as in Suggestion 1!)

3. **When you teach academic writing, assign writing topics that require making and supporting a claim based on data.**

   If we want students to practice manipulating language for arguments in academic writing, we have to give assignments that elicit that kind of argumentation. Personal narrative topics and social issues with distinct pro and con positions do not. Some teachers believe it is easier to start writing with personal topics, but as students advance they need to make a transition to writing as it is more likely to be practiced in academic disciplines. We need to give students practice with language for analyzing data, for appropriately stating claims and interpretations, and for supporting them. The first step is to assign appropriate writing tasks.

Data can include numbers or be qualitative, and they can be related to any field. You can profitably make use of any background or hobbies that you have. Since I have a background in biology, I have designed writing assignments that asked my ESL students to gather and analyze data on biological topics. For example, in a high-intermediate to advanced ESL class, I had students do a small analysis of different kinds of plants, analyzing how samples I gave them were adapted to dry or wet conditions. They had to complete a table of information and write up their analysis, much like a lab report. A number of my ESL students came back later to tell me that the science writing practice proved very helpful once they were regular university students fulfilling distribution requirements, but you do not need to use scientific topics to give students practice with data analysis. Even many popular activities in ESL classes, such as interviewing Americans on a given topic, can be taken to the next step for writing practice: ask students to put the information into a table, analyze it, and make an interpretation that they support. If your ESL students ask Americans whether or not they are religious and why, for example, you can ask your students to compile all their answers and sort them into categories. Then ask students to describe each category and give an example of a typical comment, filling in a table such as this:

Category	Number of Respondents	Description	Example Comment
dislike organized religion	5	These people think of themselves as connected to God but they do not like institutions and rules.	"I think of myself as spiritual but not religious."
identify with a particular religion but do not attend regularly	4	These people say they belong to a certain religion but they rarely go to services.	"I'm Catholic, but I only go to Mass on Christmas and Easter."

Writing a paper to describe the categories students have found, exemplify them, and make some tentative interpretations about Americans' religious practices is useful practice for analytical writing.

4. **To help students develop their awareness of how to adapt language for different academic contexts, give assignments that have students analyze writing in different disciplines and for different audiences.**

In ESL writing classes, it is impossible to teach students about all the types of writing they may do as regular students in the university. However, it is possible to teach them tools for analyzing writing to see how certain functions are fulfilled in a discipline. Use the findings of corpus-based studies to help you focus students on important language differences. I have, for example, focused students on verb tense as they compare how methods are described in different disciplines. I have also had students analyze the language used to express an opinion as they compare a research article and popular magazine article on the same topic. I have also asked students to compare the most common recurring expressions in professional writing versus student writing, as described in the study by Cortes (2004).

One of my most successful analysis tasks for students has been asking them to compare a small part of one history article written by a professional historian and one history paper written by an undergraduate student. Both are biographies, with the goal of connecting a person's life to historical events. The opening paragraphs are as follows:

Article from a history journal: *Josephine Baker, Racial Protest, and the Cold War*

During the early 1950s, Josephine Baker was an international star who lived in a castle in France, who wore Dior gowns in concert, and whose most radical political idea seems to have been a hope that the world might some day live in racial harmony. She would hardly seem a threat to the national security of the United States. Nevertheless, during the early fifties, the Federal Bureau of Investigation (FBI) kept a file on Baker, and the State Department collected data on her activities, using the information to dissuade other countries from allowing her to perform. Baker was seen as a threat because she used her international prominence to call attention to the discriminatory racial practices of the United States, her native land, when she traveled throughout the world.

(Dudziak, 1994, p. 543)

Student paper: *My Grandmother the Magic Maker*

People have such an amazing effect on things. If you take a great class, you don't remember what you learned, you remember the person who taught it to you. You can look at photographs and seeing someone's face can remind you of a thousand times you've shared with that person. Everyday, around the world, people are doing and experiencing things and telling other people about them. There is so much to learn from people—ideas, experiences, memories, heartaches. Each and every story you tell or listen to becomes a part of you, something that you can relate to something in your present life, or something that will happen in the future. It is important to share these ideas and memories and tears with others so they can share your joy or anger or frustration. The following essay is memories recounted to me and now I will share them with you.

One task I ask students to do is compare the use of nouns and pronouns. Immediately students notice that the undergraduate paper has expressions with a vague *you: if you take a great class, you can look at photographs*. As they read analytically, the students themselves see how ineffective this use of *you* is when the audience for the paper is a professor. The professor isn't taking a class, and the professor certainly doesn't want to hear that no one remembers what was learned in a class! Although the student writer may have been attempting to make the paper more personally engaging, this technique was not effective. They notice that the student's very first noun is a vague *people*. The professional, on the other hand, states the name *Josephine Baker* in the opening sentence. Other proper nouns include other important characters in the biography—the FBI, the State Department.

In these introductions I also ask students to identify where they see historical context appearing. My students notice that the very first phrase in the professional's article *(During the early 1950s)* provides the historical period, but this is lacking in the student writer's opening. I also focus the students on how the professional historian expresses her main idea: *Baker was seen as a threat because.* This past tense sentence is the author's main claim, and the rest of the article offers support for it.

Interestingly, my students' first reaction is often that the professional text is boring and the student writing more interesting. After we look more closely at the language and the goal of a biography in history (connecting a person to historical events), most students come to see the professional text as artful and the student writer as ineffective. As one of my students summed up the student writer's introductory paragraph after analyzing the language choices, "If the teacher said write a biography and connect to history, where's the biography and where's the history?"

5. **Learn about other disciplines from faculty in them, and then relate what they tell you to your own analyses of the writing.** Being an effective teacher of academic writing means getting to know a variety of academic disciplines. While it is useful for students to interview faculty about writing in the field they want to major in, I have found that there is no substitute for going to talk with other faculty myself. We all already have too much to do and too little time to do it in, but even four fifteen-minute

talks with faculty in different departments will allow you to understand language differences across disciplines more clearly. And although I found it daunting at first to interview other faculty about writing, I have discovered that most people—after their initial surprise and occasional denial of knowing anything about good writing—are very happy to have someone show interest. Questions that have worked well for me include:

1. What kinds of writing assignments do students do in your department?
2. What are the most important skills for students to have for doing those assignments well?
3. What are the most common writing problems that you see international students having?
4. What usually frustrates you the most when you are grading a large stack of papers?
5. How did *you* learn to write in your discipline? What was the hardest thing for you to learn?
6. What do you think sets apart the writing in your discipline from other disciplines in the university?

Of course, few people are as analytically aware of language as ESL teachers, so you will have to work to turn some comments into language information. I have had a number of colleagues tell me students just need to "write clearly," and it has taken a number of other questions and my own analyses to learn what that means for their discipline. It might be helpful to ask faculty to talk through the strengths and weaknesses of a particular student paper with you. For example, I once heard a biology teacher complain about a student paper ending with *I hope one day we will know for sure.* As the instructor put it, "I keep saying in class how, in science, we never really know anything *for sure!*" As an ESL teacher who knew about language use, I could then turn that comment into a language lesson: If in science you don't want to sound absolutely certain of interpretations for research, what language do you use to hedge appropriately, stating something with enough certainty but not too much? To raise students' awareness of how professionals deal with this challenge, lessons with lexical bundles are useful here. You could, for example, have students look at how these lexical bundles are used in a collection of science articles: What section (Introduction, Methods, Results, or Discussion) do they most often occur in? What are they used with: descriptions of data, explanations for findings, or statements emphasizing importance? (Generally, it is the explanations for findings that are hedged.)

Typical Lexical Bundles for Hedging

it is possible that

it is likely that

it may be that

may be due to

is/are likely to be

does not seem to be

does not appear to be

these results suggest that

---

6. **Don't emphasize creative language use at the expense of typical, useful lexical bundles or common words.**

Many of us entered the field of ESL teaching because we have a love of language, and we enjoy the beauty of an original, well-turned phrase. For academic writing, however, giving readers the wording that they expect is efficient and effective. While a judicious use of creative language can make ideas clearer and more memorable, students' proficiency also increases from using the typical lexical bundles.

How will you be able to know common words and typical lexical bundles in academic writing? Consult the publications in Section 3 of Figure 6.1 and other corpus-based investigations. Then you can choose to introduce lexical bundles to students in any number of ways. For example, you might introduce a small number of bundles for a certain function as it is appropriate for a specific assignment. When giving students an assignment that asks them to summarize data from studies, you introduce a few of the bundles that show that an idea is based on research (such as *have been shown to* and *studies have shown that*). As students revise their papers, ask them to consciously think about whether these expressions fit an idea that they have expressed with other words. You can also have students look for the bundles in readings or in a search on the Internet to see what kinds of contexts they are used in. Alternatively, you can have students compare the use of certain bundles in their own writing and in proficient writers' writing. A particularly powerful way to do this is to ask students to do their own corpus analyses, which leads to my next suggestion.

7. **Learn more about corpus linguistics techniques, and try some corpus analysis of your own (with or without your students).**
   Many people find that as they read more about corpus studies, they get ideas for studies they want to do themselves. This is, in fact, what happened to me. I read about a corpus-based study of academic prose generally, and I became interested in finding out more about how language choices differ across academic disciplines because of my own experience writing for different disciplines.

   Learning to do some basic corpus searches with *concordancers* (a common type of corpus software) is easy, and the software is relatively inexpensive or even free. More and more teachers are also finding that students benefit from doing searches of corpora, discovering for themselves typical language patterns and being able to correct their own errors. Comparing their own writing to the writing of more proficient writers is very motivating to some students. Plus, the students learn analytical techniques that they can apply long after their ESL classes are finished. If you are interested in learning more about how ESL students have reacted to doing corpus linguistics, you might be interested in articles by Gaskell and Cobb (2004), Yoon and Hirvela (2004), and Fan and Xu (2006) as well as many other publications that are now available.

   Doing corpus-based work yourself is useful because you know your students and their needs the best. However, it can be very time-consuming both to compile a corpus and to design new activities. Even if you use articles that you download from the web and have students send you electronic copies of their papers, you will spend a great deal of time just labeling texts and checking for problems and organizing the files. When you make activities, finding the best examples, sequencing exercises logically, and writing instructions clearly all take time. Instead of trying to do it all alone, I have found that teamwork is essential. Your students can be part of your team; some teachers make a mini-corpus of a writing assignment completed by their own students, or they have each student download or scan an article to contribute to a corpus of professional writing. The corpus grows as each class group contributes to it. Other teams consist of groups of teachers from the same program who work together to compile a corpus for their program. Where I work, for example, various instructors and teacher-trainees are working to compile The Portland State Viking Corpus of Academic Student Writing—a corpus of student writing from throughout the university that received at least a B grade; ESL teachers and students will be able to use it in writing (and grammar) classes to study how proficient writers manipulate words and grammar to fulfill the writing tasks in classes here.

Much can be said about how to use a corpus as well as how to design your own corpus. Here I mean only to whet your appetite. As you get more into corpus linguistics, a variety of books and articles are available to guide you. A good place to start is with these websites:

FIGURE 6.3. Further Information about Corpus Linguistics

For general information and links to more specialized topics within corpus linguistics:	(1) David Lee's *Bookmarks for Corpus-based Linguists*— *http://devoted.to/corpora* (2) Yvonne Breyer's *Gateway to Corpus Linguistics*— *www.corpus-linguistics.de/index.html*
For examples of teaching materials that have been developed from corpus analysis:	(1) Tim John's *Data-driven Learning Page*— *www.eisu2.bham.ac.uk/johnstf/timconc.htm* (2) Instructional materials from the Michigan Corpus of Academic Spoken English (MICASE)— *www.lsa.mich.edu/eli/micase/teaching.htm* (3) Tom Cobb's *The Compleat Lexical Tutor*—*www.lextutor.ca/*

Corpus-based work is especially useful for ESL teachers since it tells us how common or unusual specific language choices are. Even if you've thought of statistical or computer-assisted research as too complicated in the past, don't be afraid to use corpus-based research to help you become a more effective writing teacher.

Questions for Reflection

1. Look at several ESL writing textbooks. What topics or assignments are given for "writing to persuade" or "writing to make an argument"? How likely are these topics to elicit the type of "persuasion" that academic writing usually demands? Which of the topics would you use if you were teaching from these textbooks? How would you supplement the books' topics?

2. Think about one of your hobbies or interests. What type of data could be gathered about this topic? Design a writing assignment that asks students to collect, analyze, and interpret data on this topic. (Remember, analysis does not have to include counting. Analysis can be qualitative, asking students to summarize categories of data descriptively.)

3. Based on your intuition and experience, what other formulaic language chunks (or "lexical bundles") would you guess exist in academic writing (or in another context)? Use an internet search engine to see how many occurrences of these lexical bundles you find. Are they used in the types of texts that you expected? (If you have access to a corpus, search the corpus instead of the Internet.)

4. Some writing teachers believe that their role is to help students learn to write more creatively and personally, and to find their own voices. How would you counter this belief with information from this chapter and from your own experiences, if appropriate?

5. Many teachers argue that, because they cannot become experts in all academic disciplines, they must ignore variation in the way that language is used, and they try to teach a "general English." Instead of subscribing to that belief, list all the ideas you can think of for making students aware of language differences in academic disciplines without your becoming an expert in any new discipline.

6. List at least three ideas for applying the concepts covered in this chapter to a context other than academic writing. For example, if you think of a business English context, you might suggest teachers find out any lexical bundles that are common in certain types of business writing.

References

Albers, S. (2007). *The Viking corpus project documentation*. Portland, OR: Portland State University Department of Applied Linguistics.

Biber, D. (1988). *Variation across speech and writing*. Cambridge, UK: Cambridge University Press.

Biber, D., Conrad, S., & Cortes, V. (2004). *If you look at . . .* : Lexical bundles in university teaching and textbooks. *Applied Linguistics, 25,* 371–405.

Biber, D., Conrad, S., Reppen, R., Byrd, P., & Helt, M. (2002). Speaking and writing in the university: A multi-dimensional comparison. *TESOL Quarterly, 36*(1), 9–48.

Biber, D., Johansson, S., Leech, G., Conrad, S., & Finegan, E. (1999). *The Longman grammar of spoken and written English*. Harlow, UK: Pearson Education.

Conrad, S. (1996). Investigating academic texts with corpus-based techniques: An example from biology. *Linguistics and Education, 8,* 299–326.

———. (2001). Variation among disciplinary texts: A comparison of textbooks and journal articles in biology and history. In S. Conrad & D. Biber (Eds.), *Multi-dimensional studies of register variation in English* (pp. 94–107). Harlow, UK: Pearson Education.

Cortes, V. (2004). Lexical bundles in published and student disciplinary writing: Examples from history and biology. *English for Specific Purposes, 23,* 397–423.

Fan, M., & Xu, F. (2006). Enhancing the learning of business English using corpora—a case study. *IATEFL/BESIG Business Issues, 1,* 6–8.

Gaskell, D., & Cobb, T. (2004). Can learners use concordancer feedback for writing errors? *System, 32,* 301–319.

Granger, S. (1998). Prefabricated patterns in advanced EFL writing: Collocations and formulae. In A. Cowrie (Ed.), *Phraseology: Theory, analysis, and applications* (pp. 145–160). Oxford, UK: Oxford University Press.

Stoller, F., Jones, J., Costanza-Robinson, M., & Robinson, M. (2005). Demystifying disciplinary writing: A case study in the writing of chemistry. *Across the disciplines: Interdisciplinary perspectives on language, learning and academic writing, 2.* Retrieved March 6, 2007, from http://wac.colostate.edu/atd/lds/stoller.cfm

Yoon, H., & Hirvela, A. (2004). ESL student attitudes towards corpus use in L2 writing. *Journal of Second Language Writing, 13,* 257–283.

Texts Cited in Examples

Bock, C., Bock, J., & Grant, M. (1992). Effects of bird predation on grasshopper densities in an Arizona grassland. *Ecology, 73,* 1706–1717.

Dudziak, M. (1994). Josephine Baker, racial protest, and the Cold War. *The Journal of American History, 81,* 543–570.

Flores, D. (1991). Bison ecology and bison diplomacy: The southern plains from 1800 to 1850. *The Journal of American History, 78,* 465–485.

Jaffee, D. (1991). Peddlers of progress and the transformation of the rural north, 1760–1860. *The Journal of American History, 78,* 511–535.

Prude, J. (1991). To look upon the "lower sort": Runaway ads and the appearance of unfree laborers in America, 1750–1800. *The Journal of American History, 78,* 124–159.

Academic Writing Courses Should Focus on Paragraph and Essay Development

Sharon Cavusgil
Georgia State University

In the Real World

A FEW YEARS AGO, I STARTED REQUIRING students in my writing courses to provide both hard-copy and email versions of their papers. Collecting papers in both formats allows me to provide my preferred method of feedback, via paper and pen, while also maintaining electronic files of student writing for research and curriculum development. I pleasantly discovered that as students emailed their papers, they also began to include questions and comments about the coursework. What quickly became clear, however, was that the majority of messages were rather informal and, in my opinion, inappropriate. Students—even those who seemed to grasp the concept of audience and tone when writing a paper—seemed to ignore or forget about these concepts with their electronic exchanges. Typical messages, sans salutations and apparent proofreading, looked something like this: *"hi!*

i just wanna know if u have time today, i want u to read my paper b4 its due. im attaching. thx for your time :)" One student, after missing a lesson, emailed asking if we had covered *"anything important"* and if I could email the assignment. Another student's rather demanding message read, *"have u graded final papers yet? i wanna know my grade."*

I realized that the tone and style of these messages were likely influenced by text messaging and online chat rooms, but I was irritated by the level of informality. When talking with colleagues, I learned they had similar experiences. It appeared that email may have made faculty more approachable to students, but, I wondered, at what expense?

I decided to talk with the class about my reactions to their messages. I began by explaining that when students send academic email, they should follow certain conventions that may differ from other less formal electronic messages. I explained, for example, that I expected them to address me in their messages by using my title and last name, just like they do in class. I explained that without a brief introduction, their messages sounded abrupt. I had planned on also talking about tone, style, and grammar, but before I could begin, I was bombarded with questions: *Should you begin messages with "Dear"? Is "Ms." the abbreviation for "Miss"? What if you don't know whether your instructor is a "Dr."?* It occurred to me that instead of grumbling about student messages, it was my responsibility as their writing instructor to teach academic email etiquette, along with the expectations of other writing types. Although the semester schedule was already jam-packed, I knew I must find a way to incorporate this instruction and practice into my lessons.

Email instruction is just one example of how we must expand our writing instruction. To assist our students in developing the written skills that will allow them to succeed in academic classes and beyond, we must not only teach paragraph and essay development. We must also teach students the skills and strategies needed to complete a variety of academic tasks such as taking class notes, responding to short answer or essay examination items, writing summaries and critiques, and—it seems—composing electronic messages.

What the Research Says

Over the past two decades, numerous studies by institutions such as the Educational Testing Service and faculty surveys in colleges and universities have focused on the academic literacy skills required of students in degree programs. In addition, the writing-across-the- curriculum movement, which strives to incorporate well-designed writing assignments in content courses, has increased awareness of academic tasks. Results have demonstrated that students in high schools, community colleges, and universities are assigned tasks that require various rhetorical skills. Therefore, one would think that the prime objective of composition courses would be to prepare students to successfully complete the variety of writing tasks required by content-area faculty. Yet, is this the case? And what exactly are those expectations?

In general, studies and surveys related to the academic writing demands of U.S. undergraduate students indicate that students are expected to complete a wide variety of tasks, including short answer/essay responses on tests and for class assignments, lab reports, summaries, analyses/critiques of text, one- to four-page papers, and longer research papers with bibliographies. In addition, the rhetorical skills deemed necessary to complete such tasks have been identified and include the retrieval, organization, synthesis, and analysis of information.

Students' level of preparedness for these tasks has also been analyzed. One detailed report, *Academic Literacy: A Statement of Competencies Expected of Students Entering California's Public Colleges and Universities* (Intersegmental Committee of the Academic Senates, 2002), summarizes responses from faculty of various disciplines in California regarding how well students are prepared for courses requiring reading, writing, and critical-thinking skills. According to the faculty surveyed, only one-third of the students "are sufficiently prepared for the two most frequently assigned writing tasks: analyzing information for arguments and synthesizing information from several sources" (p. 11). Figure 7.1 summarizes recent research that focuses on the range of writing tasks expected and required of college students.

FIGURE 7.1. Summary of Recent Areas of Research

Research	Among the Findings
Ginther, A., & Grant, L. (1996). *A Review of the Academic Needs of Native English-Speaking College Students in the United States.*	This review of the academic needs of college students is filled with relevant information. For instance, the authors reviewed three types of literature, including literature that focused on students' abilities in academic writing tasks and literature that addressed students' perceptions of the demands of higher education.
Intersegmental Committee of the Academic Senates. (2002). *Academic Literacy: A Statement of Competencies Expected of Students Entering California's Public Colleges and Universities.*	A survey of faculty at the University of California, the California State University, and the California Community Colleges revealed the writing, reading, and critical thinking expectations for entering college freshmen as well as faculty's perceived level of preparedness of those students. Highlights: Faculty shared their opinions on "students' ability to express their thinking clearly, accurately, and compellingly through their writing" (p. 11). Faculty responded that two-thirds of college freshmen are not adequately prepared for important academic tasks.
Meritt, M., & Wiant, F. (n.d.). *A Survey of Faculty Opinion on Student Writing at the University of San Francisco.*	A 2001 study that focused on 55 primarily undergraduate required courses revealed that the most frequently assigned tasks included "essay exam questions, research papers, and critical analyses of texts" (p. 1). The most important writing purposes were identified as "analysis, argumentation, demonstration of comprehension, followed closely by reporting of information" (p. 2).
Offen-Brown, G. (n.d.). *Does the U.C. Berkeley Faculty Care about Student Writing?*	A 1999 survey of 248 faculty revealed the types of writing assignments expected in upper-division courses. Short answer or essay examination tasks appear to be the most frequent. For courses defined as having a "significant writing component," research papers, analytical papers, and oral presentations are also assigned. Project reports, oral presentations, and lab reports are expected in courses with a lesser writing component, such as in the scientific and technical fields.
Rosenfeld, M., Courtney, R., & Fowles, M. (2004). *Identifying the Writing Tasks Important for Academic Success at the Undergraduate and Graduate Levels.*	One goal of this study was "to define a domain of writing tasks thought to be important for competent academic performance across a range of subject areas" (p. 2). At the upper-division undergraduate level, the tasks judged to be "important" or "very important" for students included citation skills; coherent organization of ideas and information; appropriate use of grammar, syntax, and mechanics; effective revision and editing skills; and ability to write precisely and concisely (p. 31).

Rosenfeld, M., Leung, S., & Oltman, P.K. (2001). *The Reading, Writing, Speaking, and Listening Tasks Important for Academic Success at the Undergraduate and Graduate Levels.*	This survey of 21 universities in the U.S. and Canada focused on tasks deemed important for success in undergraduate and graduate programs. Writing tasks considered important included "[writing] in response to an assignment and [staying] on topic without digressions or redundancies; [using] background knowledge, reference or nontext materials, personal viewpoints, and other sources appropriately to support ideas, analyze, and refine arguments; [organizing] writing in order to convey major and supporting ideas; [using] relevant reasons and examples to support a position or idea; [and demonstrating] a command of standard written English, including grammar, . . . effective sentence structure, spelling, and punctuation" (p. 49).
Schneider, B., Downey, R.G., & Pollard, J. (2002). *K-State Undergraduate Writing Requirements: A Pilot Survey and Summary Report.*	A faculty survey that identified writing requirements for 50 undergraduate courses indicated that writing tasks in content courses include short answers on tests/in-class assignments (64 percent), short papers—one to four pages (48 percent), lab reports (36 percent), and essay questions on tests (34 percent). The survey indicated that only 22 percent of the courses required research papers with bibliographies.

It seems that if ESL writing courses are going to be meaningful and useful to students, we must engage students in tasks that resemble what they are expected to do in their discipline courses and provide them with the skills to be successful in those tasks.

What We Can Do

1. **Assign tasks that require students to demonstrate their understanding of academic content.**

   One of the main purposes of writing in undergraduate discipline courses is to demonstrate knowledge of course materials. For this reason, it is important that students in English for Academic Purposes (EAP) classes be given the opportunity to respond to academic content because this requirement mirrors degree courses. That is, at all levels of language proficiency, assignments should require students to expand their writing beyond personal experience or opinion.

There are countless ESL textbooks that teach students the features of paragraph or essay development, providing models of effective writing and assigning tasks to elicit such work. Often, however, students can address these writing tasks by solely utilizing previously acquired knowledge or personal experiences. Figure 7.2 illustrates writing prompts from popular ESL textbooks designed for beginning and intermediate students:

FIGURE 7.2. Sample Writing Prompts

- Describe a national monument that is important to you. What does it look like? What feelings does the monument inspire in you?
- Write a paragraph about a brand-name product that you buy.
- What steps does a successful job applicant follow?
- When you study, do you learn more when you are rewarded or punished? Why? Explain with examples.

While there is value in these materials, EAP instructors must broaden such tasks at all proficiency levels by integrating academic text into the classroom and by assigning tasks that require the integration of source text with student-generated text. For example, when working with these kinds of prompts, students could be directed to or provided with materials from credible government or education websites, pamphlets, or print articles and then taught how to integrate source ideas as background information or supporting details. At all levels, students can be taught the basics of source integration and citation, including how to apply basic strategies for paraphrasing, quoting, and/or summarizing and how to integrate parenthetical citations at the end of sentences or begin sentences with attribution structures, such as *According to the text,* or *The article explains that. . . .*

Another way that EAP students can practice writing with academic content is through the completion of shorter writing tasks similar to those commonly assigned in discipline courses, such as short-answer discussion or test items. For example, in a college psychology course, a typical writing task requires students to respond to questions such as those in Figure 7.3.

FIGURE 7.3. Typical Psychology Writing Tasks

- What is meant by "prosocial behavior"?
- Who is Pavlov, and why is his work important?
- How does operant conditioning differ from classical conditioning?

For students to base tasks such as these on personal experience and opinion would be meaningless. Therefore, in order for students to learn realistic skills, the tasks must be grounded in content and source material.

Over the years, faculty members at Georgia State University (GSU) have collected and analyzed academic assignments and exams and have developed guidelines for composing (a) identification, (b) short answer, and (c) essay tasks. Figures 7.4 and 7.5 contain information used in EAP classes at GSU to teach identification and short-answer writing tasks. The example questions and answers come from an advanced EAP writing course that uses materials from an undergraduate psychology text. (Information on essay responses can be found in the Appendix on page 157.)

FIGURE 7.4. Identification Tasks

Type of Question: Identification
The shortest kinds of questions that require written responses are identification (or ID) questions.

- ID questions usually ask for definitions of key terms related to the content. You should also state the significance of the term (why it is important).

- ID questions may also ask for information about important people, places, or theories. In your answer, include details about their relationship to the content you are studying. For example, when identifying important researchers, explain their goals and findings. Some instructors also expect you to include dates associated with the researcher or research.

- ID responses should be about one to three sentences. Complete sentences may not be necessary; however, they are recommended to improve the clarity of your answers.

- On an exam, these questions are usually worth about 2 to 5 points.

Example Questions and Answers

1. What is a cognitive map?
   A cognitive map is a mental representation of the layout of one's environment. For example, after exploring a maze, rats can often find their way around and act as if they have learned a cognitive/mental map of the maze.

2. Hermann Ebbinghaus
   Ebbinghaus (1850–1909) was a philosopher who was interested in how we learn new verbal information. He found that the amount of information remembered depends on the time spent learning.

Scoring
For this writing class, you can earn 3 points for each ID response. Your responses will be graded as follows:

- If your answer is correct and comprehensible, you earn 3 points.

- If the content is incorrect or incomplete, 1 to 3 points are deducted.

- If your format or grammar is awkward or incorrect, 1 point is deducted.

FIGURE 7.5. Short-Answer Writing Tasks[1]

Type of Question: Short Answer
Short answer questions usually ask for more information or more complex information than ID questions. They often require a written response of approximately three to six complete sentences. They are usually called "short answer questions" although instructors may use different terms. Short answer questions:

- Ask you to compare two concepts.
- Ask you to define or explain a concept and give an example.
- Ask you to briefly describe a process or research.
- Do not require a lot of detail or explanation.
- Are usually about 5 to 10 points each on an exam.

Follow the correct format in your response:

- Begin your answer with a topic sentence that includes the key words of the question.
- Support or explain the topic sentence by providing details, such as a definition of the key term, examples, comparisons, and description.
- You might end with a closing statement that is general in nature. It is also possible to end with a prediction. However, a closing statement is not necessary.
- Write approximately three to six complete sentences.

The short-answer question usually contains words and exact instructions that guide your answer. These direction words include *define, describe, compare,* and *illustrate.* When writing your short answer, pay attention to the direction words used in the question.

Example Question and Answer
Question: How does punishment affect behavior?

Answer: Punishment affects behavior in both positive and negative ways. When punishment is immediate and consistent, it can be effective in reducing the frequency of the negative behavior. For example, a parent may be able to stop her child from throwing food when she quickly and consistently reprimands this type of behavior. However, punishing can also cause some undesirable effects. To illustrate, when people are punished for their behavior, they can begin to fear the person applying the punishment, experience increased anger and aggression, or feel depressed and helpless.

Scoring
For this writing class, your short answer responses will be graded as follows:

- Each response is worth 10 points. You can earn 6 points for content and 4 points for format and grammar.
- Correct format includes (a) including key words from the question in your topic sentence and answer, and (b) keeping to the suggested length.
- Correct grammar means your answer is understandable without any major language interference. If your answer has grammatical problems, 1 to 4 points are deducted depending on the severity of the problems.
- Sometimes, it may be difficult to determine if the content is correct because of your language use. In this case, points are deducted for both content and grammar.

---

[1] These guidelines were originally developed by Sharon Cavusgil, Gayle Nelson, and Debra Snell in 1998 and revised by Sharon Cavusgil in 2006. The content examples were adapted from Myers, D. (1996). *Exploring Psychology* (3rd ed.). New York: Worth Publishing, pp. 195–221.

Although these identification, short answer, and essay tasks (see the Appendix) can be assigned as homework or in-class activities, students should ultimately be expected to write responses in the form of an exam that resembles those in content courses. Figure 7.6 is an example test from an EAP intermediate writing course that utilizes the content from a high school environmental science text:

FIGURE 7.6. Sample Science Test Types[2]

Unit 2: Environmental Science Test
Identification Questions (3 points each)
Write a definition of each key term. Use formal definition format.

1. ecosystem
2. biotic
3. abiotic
4. organism

Short Answer Questions (10 points each)
Answer three of the following questions.

1. Describe the main components of an ecosystem and give examples of each from a particular ecosystem.
2. Explain the difference between a population and a species. Use one organism as an example in your explanation.
3. Define habitat destruction and explain two ways it can happen. In addition, describe some of the effects of habitat destruction on certain populations using examples discussed in class.
4. Explain how all organisms in an ecosystem are connected to each other in a complex web. Use an example to illustrate your explanation (you can use an example from the textbook or from your own research).

Instructional issues to consider when asking students to display content knowledge in this manner include:

- Since content faculty may not clearly identify the question type or expectations for responses, ESL students should be taught to analyze questions to determine appropriate content, format, and length of responses. For

---

[2] Thank you to Louise Gobron and Margareta Larsson, faculty in the Department of Applied Linguistics & ESL, Georgia State University, for the use of this test.

example, direction words like *prove* or *explain* will likely require more detailed responses than words like *define* or *list*. Consideration should also be given to the amount of blank space provided for the answers as well as the point value of items (e.g., a 25-point answer will likely be longer than a 10-point answer).

- When students are learning the format of such responses, include formatting details in your assignment directions. As students become more proficient, remove this scaffolding. For example, the directions for Test 1 might read, *Write short answer responses for each of the items. Your answers should be approximately three to six complete sentences.* Later in the term, the directions might simply ask students to *Write a response* or it might be titled *Short Answer.*

- In general, when evaluating students' written responses, faculty across the disciplines tend to focus more on content and less on format and language. These same expectations should be modeled in academic writing courses as well (as seen in the identification and short answer scoring details provided previously).

2. **Assist students in understanding that writing takes a variety of forms and that many skills are transferable**.

A transferable skill is one that you take with you to other experiences. For example, some of the organizational skills that someone uses to manage a home can be transferred to the workplace. ESL teachers must help students see what various writing tasks have in common and persuade them that these writing strategies can be applied across assignments and courses. For example, in the ESL classroom, demonstrate how the features of effective paragraph development should also be applied to a typical short essay examination response. In addition, help students understand the purpose of taking reading notes and teach the skills to accomplish this task. Then explain that, when taken properly, reading notes can be used later in a summary or a paraphrase.

One way to help students understand the transfer of skills acquired in the ESL writing class is to ask them to share assignments from their discipline classes that require a written response. In class, analyze these assignments, discussing the method of development and possible length of response expected. Highlight similarities in tasks across the disciplines whenever possible. For instance, this writing task was provided by an ESL student enrolled in a college biology course. The student explained that each week, students in the class were assigned to research and write a short response to several questions provided by the instructor.

Assignment

What do medical professionals say about the use of cell phones and cancer? What are they basing their claims on? Please list the websites where you got your information.

Student Response

Medical professionals say that the relationship between cell phone and cancer is too weak and sometimes it doesn't even exist. According to a study from the American Health Foundation, there is no relationship between hours or years persons used cell phones with their cancer. Rather, they found that when person developed tumors, it was more often on the other side of the head than where they held the phone. They are basing their claims on the following studies and research: *http://healthlink.mcw.edu/article/950 308896.html* and *http://healthlibrary.epnet.com.*

A discussion occurred in the writing course about the similarities (and differences) between this assignment and others completed by students, including the following observations:

1. The instructor's directions and the direction words *(what, list)* indicated that the response did not require a lot of detail; it is considered a short answer response.
2. The response begins with a restatement of the key words of the question.
3. Attribution to the source information is included.
4. Many students felt that more detail was needed regarding the basis of claims. (The student later reported that the biology instructor also asked for more detail.)

The transfer of skills also applies to academic email. ESL teachers should teach that the concept of audience and tone that is important in formal academic writing transfers to the e-mail exchanges students may have with faculty and staff (and also in many workplaces). The writing teacher can set guidelines for proper etiquette of email exchanges, explaining the information that students must include in their academic messages (e.g., name and course, purpose of the email, and brief closing). If the instructor provides students with information electronically, students should be instructed to send a brief thank you. To encourage proper etiquette, ESL teachers can include this expectation in the course grade, perhaps as part of the daily assignment percentage or class participation. Figure 7.7 shows excerpts from a handout on email etiquette.

FIGURE 7.7. Email Guidelines

Using Email in the Academic Environment
When sending an email to faculty or staff in an academic environment, follow these general guidelines:

1. **Indicate your topic in the subject line.**
   Subject lines help receivers recognize the topic of your message, so include a clear subject line (e.g., MW Academic Writing absence). If you are responding to a previous message, be sure to revise the subject line if appropriate.

2. **Include an appropriate opening and closing.**
   Most writers do not use *Dear* in their email openings. However, you should begin with the person's title and last name, followed by a comma. Also, conclude your message with a brief closing, such as *Thank you*. Many students adopt a style similar to conversations in their electronic communications, including openings like *Hi, how are you?* However, this style can be considered too informal for academic email.

3. **Avoid using special symbols.**
   Generally, avoid using special symbols like :(or ^0^ in your academic email messages. They are usually considered too informal.

4. **Check that you can e-mail attachments.**
   Many instructors accept only hard copies of class work. Before you email assignments, ask your instructor if this is acceptable. If you do send an attachment, include a brief message identifying yourself and the assignment. Example:

   Dear Ms. Wald,

   This is Jana Patel from your MW writing course. I was unable to come to class today, so as you instructed, I am attaching my homework assignment—page 20 in our textbook.

   Thank you.

While many skills are transferable to other tasks and courses, it is important to make students aware of skills that must be slightly revised depending on the task, such as citation formatting. For example, while a research paper may require writers to utilize a formal documentation style like APA or MLA, an in-class written response may only require general attribution to a source, such as *According to one study.* . . . In addition, in a written assignment completed at home, extensive paraphrasing is expected. However, with in-class writing tasks, like exam responses, faculty may accept the inclusion of short memorized phrases.

3. **Integrate smaller tasks into your writing course that lead up to longer assignments.**

   To aid the transfer of skills, it is important to integrate various shorter tasks into the ESL writing class that build into larger academic tasks. A series of shorter writing tasks can allow students to strengthen writing skills while building content knowledge to be used later in longer assignments. For example, instead of assigning a few longer research papers during a term, consider assigning more numerous one- to two-page assignments that require students to integrate information from several sources. In doing so, they may be exposed to essential academic skills, like synthesizing, more often. The following illustrate ways to expand on the traditional research component found in many ESL writing courses by integrating practice with other essential academic writing tasks.

   - If your course textbook does not include academic content readings, provide students with one or two credible sources. To avoid copyright issues, leave the sources at your library reserve desk or provide Internet information for individual student retrieval.
   - Use the content readings as models of academic text (e.g., as examples of paragraph development, use of supporting information, or attribution of expert opinions).

- As a class, predict potential "content" questions that might stem from the readings. That is, ask students to predict what a content instructor might want them to know about the material. Utilize existing discussion questions from the textbook, if possible. (You may need to integrate reading and note-taking strategies into the discussion.)
- Categorize the predicted content questions as requiring identification, short answer, or essay responses. Then, have students respond to these questions orally, taking notes during the discussion (and perhaps adding to or clarifying their reading notes). Following the oral discussion, ask students to explore the topic by drafting identification, short answer, and short essay responses. These oral and written tasks help students develop their knowledge and vocabulary understanding within the content area.
- At this point, move into the research component of the course. Require students to use some of the content knowledge acquired in class and that has already been summarized, paraphrased, and/or analyzed, along with new information they investigate on their own. The idea is that, through the discussion and initial drafting, students will have acquired a knowledge base about the topic, and as a result, the research component will seem less overwhelming. After all, they are now investigating to fill in gaps in their knowledge.
- About the time their research paper is due, give students a test that resembles those found in content courses. Assess both their understanding of the content (about 60 percent of their grade) and the format and language of expected responses (about 40 percent of their grade).

In English composition courses for undergraduate ESL students at GSU, these steps are repeated approximately every five weeks, allowing students to cover three content units in a fifteen-week semester.

To ensure that EAP writing courses are meaningful and useful, students must be given the opportunity to respond to and incorporate content information through a variety of writing tasks resembling the requirements found in discipline courses. These authentic tasks should include not only paragraph and research writing, but also note-taking, email correspondence, and responses to identification, short answer, and essay discussion/exam questions. Such practice can occur in frequent, shorter tasks that lead up to or even replace longer assignments. In addition, by encouraging students to share and discuss their own experiences and knowledge of content faculty expectations, EAP courses will help foster the successful transfer of essential writing skills to degree coursework.

Questions for Reflection

1. Discuss your understanding of the reading and writing tasks content-area faculty (high school, college, undergraduate or graduate) expect students to complete. How might you develop or improve your knowledge of these expectations? How might such knowledge influence your own teaching of writing?

2. Consider an EAP writing course you teach (or may have to teach). What are the prime objectives of that course? Discuss how these objectives prepare students to successfully complete writing tasks required by content-area faculty. How might these objectives be revised or improved to better prepare students for future expectations?

3. One suggestion offered in this chapter is to assign tasks in EAP writing courses that require students to demonstrate their understanding of academic content. This means that, at all levels of language proficiency, assignments should require students to expand their writing beyond personal experience or opinion. Discuss how this suggestion might be implemented in a lower-proficiency level writing course.

4. Consider a writing course you are familiar with. Review or locate academic content that is or could be used in the course. Using the material, brainstorm two to three potential identification and short answer questions and answers. Discuss the processes you followed to identify and complete these questions and appropriate responses.

5. Consider a writing course that you teach or may have to teach that incorporates research writing. How might you integrate smaller tasks into this course that lead up to the longer research writing assignments?

Special thanks to my colleague and friend, John Stowe, for his camaraderie, support, and contagious enthusiasm for teaching.

6. To ensure that EAP writing courses are meaningful and useful, students must be given the opportunity to respond to and incorporate content information through a variety of writing tasks resembling the requirements found in discipline courses. What might be the biggest obstacles to incorporating content into writing courses? How might you overcome these obstacles?

References

CSUS faculty writing survey results. (2002). Writing across the curriculum, California State University, Sacramento. (2002). Retrieved January 3, 2006, from http://www.csus.edu/wac/survey.htm

Ginther, A., & Grant, L. (1996). *A review of the academic needs of native English-speaking college students in the United States.* TOEFL Monograph Series. Princeton, NJ: Educational Testing Service. RM-96-4.

Intersegmental Committee of the Academic Senates. (2002). *Academic literacy: A statement of competencies expected of students entering California's public colleges and universities.* Washington, DC: U.S. Department of Education. ED-469-982.

Meritt, M., & Wiant, F. (n.d.). *A survey of faculty opinion on student writing at the University of San Francisco.* Retrieved February 13, 2006, from http://www.usfca.edu/rhetcomp/survey.html

Myers, D. (1996). *Exploring psychology* (3rd ed.) (pp. 195–221). New York: Wadsworth.

Offen-Brown, G. (n.d.). *Does the U.C. Berkeley faculty care about student writing?* Retrieved January 2, 2006, from http://www-writing.berkeley.edu/wab/1-1-does.htm

Rosenfeld, M., Courtney, R., & Fowles, M. (2004). *Identifying the writing tasks important for academic success at the undergraduate and graduate levels.* GRE Board Report No. 00-04-R, ETS RR-04-42.

Rosenfeld, M., Leung, S., & Oltman, P. K. (2001). *The reading, writing, speaking, and listening tasks important for academic success at the undergraduate and graduate levels.* TOEFL Monograph Series. Princeton, NJ: Educational Testing Service. RM-01-03.

Schneider, B., Downey, R.G., & Pollard, J. (2002). *K-State undergraduate writing requirements: A pilot survey and summary report.* Manhattan: Kansas State University Office of Planning and Analysis. Research Report #86.

Zhu, W. (2004). Faculty views on the importance of writing, the nature of academic writing, and teaching and responding to writing in the disciplines. *Journal of Second Language Writing, 13*(1), 29–48.

Appendix

Type of Question: Essay

Students in academic classes are often asked to respond to essay questions, either as an assignment or on an exam. Essay questions ask students to explain more complex ideas than ID or short answer questions, and students need to write more sentences. Essay questions usually ask students to

- Explain a concept, event, or procedure in detail. You should provide accurate examples to prove or support your ideas.
- Show the relationship between two or more concepts, events, or procedures (e.g., cause/effect, compare/contrast, classification).
- Summarize the main points of or describe an idea, invention, event, or theory.
- Discuss the importance or advantages/disadvantages of an idea, invention, event, or theory.

On an exam, these questions are usually worth from 15 to 30 points.

The most important part in answering an essay question is that your information is correct. However, you must also follow the correct form in your response:

- Begin your answer with a topic sentence that includes the key words of the question.
- Support or explain the topic sentence and main point(s) by defining key terms and providing details, examples, comparisons, and so forth.
- You do not necessarily need a conclusion. However, you may need to end with a general statement that restates your main idea.
- For a short essay, write approximately eight to fifteen complete sentences.
- For a longer essay, write approximately three to five paragraphs.

Directions for essay questions usually contain words and exact instructions that guide your answer (e.g., *define, what is, compare*). When writing your essay, you must pay attention to the language used in the question.

Example Question and Answer

Question: What are the basic types of reinforcers?

Answer: A reinforcer is anything (e.g., a reward, praise, an activity) that increases or strengthens a behavior. For example, earning a high grade is a reinforcer because when students earn a high grade, they are likely to be motivated to continue studying. There are different types of reinforcers. Reinforcers can be positive or negative. A positive reinforcer strengthens a response by providing a positive stimulus like money, attention, or approval. A negative reinforcer is the removal of an unpleasant stimulus, like when a person stops whining or yelling. Reinforcers can also be primary or secondary. Primary reinforcers are innate. They satisfy a biological need, like food. Secondary reinforcers—like money or a pleasant tone of voice—are learned or conditioned. Finally, reinforcers can be immediate or delayed. As the words indicate, a behavior can be reinforced immediately (clapping, a smile) or it can be delayed (receiving a paycheck at the end of the month). Regardless of the type, all reinforcers strengthen the behaviors that they follow. (14 complete sentences)

Scoring

For this writing class, you can earn 25 points for each essay response. Your responses will be graded as follows:

- You can earn up to 10 points for content. Your content score will be determined based on the completeness and accuracy of the content information you provide. Your answer should be fully developed with specific facts and examples.

- You can earn up to 10 points for organization. Your organization score will be determined based on your development, organization, and coherence. In addition, you should restate the question accurately.

- You can earn up to 5 points for language use. Your language score will be determined based on the accuracy and use of academic vocabulary and structures, accurate use of a variety of sentence types, accurate use of word forms and verb tenses, and source text language that is well integrated with student-generated language.

MYTH 8

International and U.S. Resident ESL Writers Cannot Be Taught in the Same Class

Paul Kei Matsuda
Arizona State University

In the Real World

A FEW YEARS AGO, AT THE END OF A TESOL COLLOQUIUM on ESL writing issues, a teacher in the audience—I'll call her Elizabeth—raised her hand and asked whether international and resident ESL students should be taught in the same class. She explained that her institution had been sending resident ESL students to her class, which traditionally had included only international students who came directly from their home countries. After the colloquium, she approached some of the presenters, including me, and the conversation continued in the hallway until well into the next session. It seemed clear from her tone that she was frustrated by the challenge of working with different groups of students who had vastly differing needs, characteristics, and attitudes, and she seemed to be asking the ESL writing experts on the panel to assure her that her institution was wrong in sending resident students to her ESL writing class.

Elizabeth is not alone. I have heard other ESL writing teachers voice the same concerns. In fact, I had a similar reaction when I first taught a section of first-year composition for international students. When two resident ESL students showed up at the beginning of the semester asking me—in impeccable English—to sign them into my ESL writing course, I told them they did not need to be in an ESL section. Not fully aware of the issues surrounding resident ESL writers, I turned them away to make room for two international students who, I thought, more desperately needed my course. Even today, I sometimes wonder about the fate of the two resident ESL students.

Although resident ESL students have been part of U.S. higher education as early as the mid-1950s (Slager, 1956), this population of students has not been studied extensively, especially in the context of ESL classrooms that have been dominated by international students. In recent years, however, the demographic and sociolinguistic changes have resulted in changes in the college student population, and a growing number of resident ESL students are being sent to ESL classes of various types and levels. Yet addressing their needs in those classes have been difficult for a number of reasons. The relative lack of information about the new population and how to address their needs is certainly one. Another seems to be the persistence of the myth that international and U.S. resident ESL writers cannot be taught in the same class.

By calling it a myth, I am not suggesting that *all* resident ESL students can or should be placed with international ESL students. I would be concerned about such an extreme position, especially when the argument is motivated by the financial need of the ESL program rather than the needs of the resident and international ESL students (Leki, 1991). The goal of this chapter is to address the other extreme position: That *no* resident ESL students should ever be placed with international ESL students.

What the Research Says and Shows

As a traditionally trained ESL writing teacher with years of experience in teaching international students, Elizabeth recognized that the needs of resident ESL writers were not being met in her class. However, research does seem to support Elizabeth's key assumptions: (a) International ESL students and resident ESL students are often different, and (b) ESL writing programs are not designed to address the needs of international students.

International and Resident ESL Students Are Often Different ——

Although much of what we know about teaching academic writing to ESL students is based on international ESL students, there is a growing body of research to suggest that international and resident ESL students have differing needs. Various terms have been used to highlight the distinction between the two groups of students:

Resident ESL Students	International ESL Students
immigrant students	foreign students (Slager, 1956)
bilingual minority students	foreign students (Valdés, 1992)
immigrant students	international students (Williams, 1995)
ear learners	eye learners (Reid, 1998)
generation 1.5 students	international students (Harklau, Losey, & Siegal, 1999)

Some of these categories are not fully compatible because they are based on different criteria, but they do overlap to a large extent, with the immigration status explicitly or implicitly serving as the basis for distinction.

As many ESL teachers and authors readily acknowledge, these categories are not as clear-cut as they may seem at first; there are many factors that are involved in identifying student profiles. At the same time, these categories usefully highlight the presence of a growing number of resident ESL students whose needs have not been addressed in ESL writing classrooms. Some of the salient generalizations about this resident population include the following; they

- have been educated in U.S. schools for at least several years
- learned English through informal spoken interactions
- are fluent in informal spoken English
- have limited metalinguistic knowledge of English
- transfer oral features into writing (e.g., spelling errors, colloquialisms)
- are aware of U.S. youth culture
- show strong integrative motivation
- are resistant to being grouped with international students
- may have limited L1 literacy
- may have had their education interrupted
- may self-identify as fully bilingual or even native English speakers

While not all resident ESL writers share these characteristics, a combination of some of these features seem to set them apart from typical international students (Chiang & Schmida, 1999; Harklau, Siegal, & Losey, 1999; Leki, 1991; Reid, 1998; Slager, 1956; Valdés, 1992; Williams, 1995).

Traditional ESL Writing Courses Are Designed for International Students ——

ESL courses at many U.S. colleges and universities—whether they are part of intensive English programs or parallel ESL sections of mainstream composition courses—were not originally designed to address the needs of resident ESL students. This is because resident ESL students did not have a strong presence in the formative years of ESL and ESL writing courses—between the 1910s and 1960s (Matsuda, 1999,

2003a, 2003b, 2006). In U.S. higher education, the foundation for current structures for ESL courses and programs were developed during the early half of the 20th century, when the ESL students were predominantly international students who were educated in their own countries and who came to the United States as sojourners. In fact, one of the most influential models for the intensive English program, created in 1941 at the English Language Institute (ELI) at the University of Michigan, was initially designed for international graduate students from Latin American countries. Although the scope of intensive English programs expanded to serve a growing international student population after World War II, those programs did not focus on serving the differing needs of resident ESL writers (Slager, 1956).

In the 1960s and 1970s, the number of resident ESL students began to increase rapidly as a result of the changes in the immigration law as well as the advent of open admissions at many urban institutions and community colleges. By that time, however, the assumption of ESL students as international students had already been firmly established. Although many open admissions institutions—most notably the City University of New York—developed ESL courses that served both resident and international ESL students, issues surrounding resident ESL writers did not receive significant attention in the mainstream TESOL literature or in ESL teacher education programs for decades (Matsuda, 2003a). Toward the end of the 1990s, the presence and needs of resident ESL writers began to gain recognition among a growing number of ESL writing teachers and researchers (see Harklau, Losey, & Siegal, 1999), but ESL writing programs and teacher education programs are only beginning to explore the implications of the changing demographics.

Complicating the Scenario ——

The research seems to support Elizabeth's premises about the differing needs, characteristics, and attitudes that international and resident ESL students tend to bring with them. The research also supports her premise that her course was not originally designed to address the needs of resident ESL writers (Leki, 1999; Reid, 1998; Roy, 1984). It may seem reasonable, then, for Elizabeth to conclude that resident ESL students should not be placed into her ESL writing course. Addressing this issue, however, may not be as simple as placing resident ESL students elsewhere because research also suggests that Elizabeth's conclusion may be untenable.

Placement Options ——

First, if resident ESL writers are not placed in an ESL writing classes, where are they supposed to go? At most U.S. institutions of higher education, other possible placement options include mainstream sections of first-year composition and basic (also known as developmental) writing (Silva, 1994). While some arguments have been made in favor of integrating ESL writers into basic writing courses (e.g., Roy, 1984, 1988), others (e.g., Benson, Deming, Denzer, & Valeri-Gold, 1992; Braine, 1996) have argued against placing ESL writers with NES students because those sections are not always designed with ESL writers—resident or international—in mind. While advanced ESL writers may benefit from mainstreaming—especially if the teacher is prepared to work with language issues (Matsuda & Silva, 1999), a majority of mainstream composition teachers and basic writing teachers are only beginning to understand that they may need to think about addressing ESL writers' needs in their classrooms (Matsuda, 1999, 2003a, 2003b; Valdés, 1992; Williams, 1995). For that reason, mainstream and basic writing courses may not provide an ideal placement solution for all resident ESL writers.

At many urban institutions and two-year colleges whose missions are to provide greater access to college education, resident ESL students often outnumber international ESL students or, in some cases, even NES students in the writing classroom (Matsuda, 2003a). At those institutions, international and resident ESL writers have long been integrated into the same course. While more traditional types of ESL writing courses can certainly be modified to fit this model, there is not enough research to suggest the exact nature of modification or how this model might help ESL writing courses with a small number of resident ESL writers. Yet, the existence of those programs suggests that teaching resident and international ESL students together is not altogether unrealistic. It is also important to note that teachers who teach at those institutions have had to take it upon themselves to retrain themselves to work with an increasingly diverse student population (Shaughnessy, 1976).

Some institutions have developed what Silva (1994) has called a *cross-cultural composition* course—a course that systematically integrates U.S. and international students together. If taught by teachers who have preparation and experience in teaching both mainstream and ESL writing courses, this option can create some room for identity negotiation for resident ESL students, who may identify themselves as U.S. students or even native English speakers (Chiang & Schmida, 1999). Matsuda and Silva (1999), for example, included three resident students—two Hindi-speaking students originally from India and one Puerto Rican whose dominant language was Spanish. The course provided flexible identity options: All of them positioned themselves as U.S. students; the Puerto Rican student, who was Spanish dominant, identified himself as a native English speaker. At some institutions, a course that includes a large number of resident and international ESL writers may already be an everyday reality. At other institutions, creating placement options is not always easy because of the difficulty of predicting enrollment, securing funding, and coordinating placement (Matsuda & Silva, 1999).

Another possibility is to create a separate course just for resident ESL writers. If it can be worked out, the course might create additional options in addressing the "ill-served needs" of resident ESL writers (Leki, 1999, p. 17). Yet, persuading institutions to create this placement option may be difficult because of the cost unless there is a steady stream of resident ESL students who can be identified as clearly distinct from both NES writers and international ESL writers. Thus, while it may work ideally for some resident students at some institutions, it may not be possible for programs at other institutions to identify and place students in these sections, which brings us to the second complicating factor: the difficulty of identifying resident ESL writers.

Identifying Resident ESL Writers ——

Despite the generalizations about resident ESL writers in the research literature that are constructed in contrast to international ESL students, individual characteristics of resident ESL writers tend to be much more complex. The category of "resident ESL writers" may include, for example, long-term U.S. residents who have lived in a minority-language community in the United States as well as students who have arrived in the last few years with parents who are faculty members at a U.S. research university (Fu, 2003).

For this reason, identifying "resident ESL writers" who might benefit from the same placement is difficult in many cases. Holistic scores from writing samples, which many institutions use for placement, do not provide sufficient information about the needs of individual students (Hamp-Lyons, 1991). Students' self identification, though insightful and meaningful in its own right, is also not always a reliable tool for placement decision because resident ESL students may be going through a complex process of negotiating their linguistic and cultural identities that defies any attempts to categorize them. In fact, many are uncomfortable with traditional categories such as "language minority" or "ESL" speakers and classify themselves as native English speakers (Chiang & Schmida, 1999).

The distinction based on the immigration status—international visa students, on the one hand and permanent residents, refugees, and naturalized and native-born citizens on the other hand—provide a less ambiguous way of classifying students. Yet, even these categories may become problematic when the characteristics of individual writers are considered. Some international students are more like resident ESL students in some ways and vice versa. Instead of seeing the difference as a dichotomy or even a continuum, it would be useful to consider students' profile in terms of a series of parallel continua, with each individual students having a unique combination of characteristics (see Figure 8.1).

FIGURE 8.1. Parallel Continua of Tendencies in Student Characteristics

	International	Resident
Content Knowledge in L1	More developed <= = = = = = = = = =>	Less developed
Content Knowledge in L2	Less developed <= = = = = = = = = =>	More developed
L2 Metalinguistic Knowledge	More developed <= = = = = = = = = =>	Less developed
L1 Literacy	More developed <= = = = = = = = = =>	Less developed
L2 Literacy	More developed <= = = = = = = = = =>	Less developed
L1 Oral Communication	More developed <= = = = = = = = = =>	Less developed
L2 Oral Communication	Less developed <= = = = = = = = = =>	More developed
Heritage Culture Knowledge	More familiar <= = = = = = = = = =>	Less familiar
Target Culture Knowledge	Less familiar <= = = = = = = = = =>	More familiar
Instrumental Motivation	Stronger <= = = = = = = = = =>	Weaker
Integrative Motivation	Weaker <= = = = = = = = = =>	Stronger
L1 Maintenance	Less difficult <= = = = = = = = = =>	More difficult

Distinguishing resident and international students, then, is not as straightforward as it may seem at first. Issues surrounding the placement of resident ESL students also depends largely on the local institutional context. At institutions that enroll a large and steady population of resident ESL students who are clearly distinguishable from international ESL students, creating a separate course for those students might be feasible. At many institutions, where the resident student population is more diverse and unpredictable, creating a separate placement may not be logistically possible or financially feasible. The limited availability of appropriate placement options at many institutions and the difficulty of identifying the needs and characteristics of the students make it difficult to come up with a one-size-fits-all solution.

What We Can Do

As explained, while there are some differences between international and resident ESL students, the difference is not always dichotomous;

rather, the differences are better understood as parallel continua of characteristics. For this reason, it is not always appropriate to determine placement based on generalizations related principally to students' immigration status. Furthermore, at many institutions, placing resident ESL writers in traditionally designed ESL writing classes is often a necessity—for the lack of alternatives or financial resources. In those situations, the responsibility is on us ESL writing teachers to do what we can to address the needs of all students who are in our classrooms.

It may mean that we need to retool our teaching repertoire and/or to redesign our curriculum. But then again, that is just what all reflective teachers should be doing all along. Teaching is not a static activity: The student population, institutional mission, and available pedagogical resources are constantly shifting, and we need to evolve with those changes as well. In order to address the needs of *all* ESL writers, everyone who teaches writing—ESL or otherwise—needs to learn to work effectively with all types of students who are in their classrooms *today*. What, then, can we do as ESL writing teachers, especially when the particular institutional context does not allow resident ESL writers to be placed elsewhere?

1. **Recognize the presence and needs of resident ESL writers.**
   The first and most obvious step is to recognize the presence of resident ESL writers. We need to become aware of the changing demographics and to accept that the nature of our job as ESL writing teachers is constantly shifting. While it is important to work toward creating better placement practices, we need to focus our attention on the students who are already in our classrooms.

   We also need to understand as much as possible about resident ESL writers—their general characteristics as well as the complex combination of characteristics that each individual student brings to the classroom. Familiarizing ourselves with a growing number of publications or attending conference sessions and workshops related to issues surrounding resident ESL writers is the necessary first step (see, for example, Harklau, Losey, & Siegal, 1999; Roberge, Siegal, & Harklau, 2008). It is important to learn the general demographics of our own institutions and surrounding communities by talking to colleagues and program administrators and by consulting the international student office and multicultural student office. Checking U.S. Census data about the demographics and the sociolinguistic context of the larger community is also important.

In the classroom, we can find out more about individual students by, for example, using a questionnaire about student's language background (for a sample questionnaire, see Reid, 1998, or see the Appendix page 175). Given the complexity of the student population, it is important to avoid phrasing questions in ways that assume simple dichotomy between L1 and L2 or NES and NNES. For example, instead of asking, *What is your native language?* we might ask, *What languages do you speak (or write)? Which languages are you most comfortable speaking (or writing)?*

Another possibility is to assign a literacy narrative (Soliday, 1994) at the beginning of the semester, either as a small in-class assignment or as the first major assignment in which students explain their L1 and L2 literacy background and experience. Or more simply, developing a literacy timeline, an outline of significant literacy or language learning events, can be useful for students at lower proficiency levels or as a starting point for more complex literacy narrative assignments. Students might also complete a learning style survey (e.g., *www.carla.umn.edu/about/profiles/CohenPapers/LearningStylesSurvey.pdf*) or study skills survey (e.g., *www.latech.edu/students/counseling/assets studyskillsquiz.pdf*).[1]

Keeping track of the student population in the classroom can help us understand how the makeup of the student population often differs from section to section and from term to term. Having a record of how many resident students are enrolled in ESL writing courses may also help us in the future if making an argument for a cross-cultural composition course or a special section for resident ESL students becomes necessary.

---

[1] Readers are reminded that URLs can change without notice.

Finding out about the students can also help make the mixed classroom of resident and international ESL writers a more productive learning space by seeing—and helping students see—the differences as resources. A simple way to accomplish this goal is to ask students to interview each other about their strengths as writers or readers and present the information to class. It can help students see beyond the apparent differences in oral proficiency or the length of stay in the United States. This type of activity can take place at the beginning of the semester or at the time of forming peer groups. It would be even more effective if we give students an opportunity to choose their peer group members based on the strengths.

2. **Learn as much as we can about our own teaching.**
Reflective teachers review, reflect on, and revise their teaching practices constantly, but it is especially important when the student demographics are changing. What we think has always worked may not be working for the new ESL student population; even international ESL student characteristics are quickly changing. For example, international students today tend to be more familiar with some aspects of U.S. linguistic and cultural practices than their predecessors because of the worldwide spread of the English language and the rise of the international youth culture, as well as the popularity of the English-dominant Internet. For this reason, we as teachers need to strive for teaching practices that address the common needs of an increasingly diverse student population while also addressing the individual needs.

Reviewing the syllabus and textbooks for the list of learning objectives—explicit or implicit—might be a good place to start. Learning objectives such as "becoming familiar with the U.S. culture and customs" or "understanding the difference between home country and the United States" might alienate some resident ESL writers who have a strong desire to identify the United States as their home. Items that are important to some students but not to others may be best addressed through teacher written feedback or individual conferences rather than as part of the main class activity. We may also reflect on how we instruct our students to avoid, for example, conflating international students and ESL students or positioning ESL students against U.S. students, which some instructors do as a way of strengthening the solidarity among ESL students.

In some classrooms, there may be a number of students whose writing needs are similar to the others but who stand out in terms of their oral communication skills. To facilitate learning for all students, it would be useful to present teaching materials, assignments, and guidelines in written form, in the form of handouts and overhead transparencies or PowerPoint slides. When available, we might also use technology resources such as Blackboard, WebCT, or a course website to make the instruction available. Such resources can reduce the amount of teacher-talk or clarification in class, and students who may take longer to process instructions would be able to study the instructions later with the help of dictionaries or tutors. We might also consider using the interactive features of technology to clarify assignments and instructions. Although writing detailed instructions may initially take time, it can save time later because the same handouts, perhaps with some revisions, can be recycled in other similar courses in the future.

Teaching is a complex act, and every teaching situation is different because of the combination of various factors, including the student population and their characteristics and needs as well as institutional and program missions, existing program structures and available resources. To complicate the matter further, all of these factors can change over time. As such, it is impossible to come up with one-size-fits-all solutions. What is important is for all of us to learn more about our students, reflect on our practices, and make adjustments to serve the needs of all students—residents or international—who are affected by our practices.

Questions for Reflection

1. Check the institution's website for the statistics published by various campus offices (e.g., international student office, multicultural student office, etc.). How many international students attend your institution? How many resident ESL students? Are there communities near your institution where languages other than English are dominant? Do the statistics match your sense of reality?

2. What language support programs are available at your local institution? If there is an intensive language program, what population of students does it serve? For resident ESL students? Is there a basic writing program? What kind of qualifications and experience do the teachers in each of these programs have? How are students identified and placed into these courses?

3. When you plan your EAP writing course, what kind of students do you imagine? Where do they come from? What language and literacy backgrounds do they bring to the classroom? How do you know?

4. How have the demographics in your classroom changed over time? How has your teaching changed over time?

5. What kinds of teaching materials do you use in your teaching? What kinds of implicit and explicit assumptions about the students' backgrounds do they make?

References

Benson, B., Deming, M. P., Denzer, D., & Valeri-Gold, M. (1992). A combined basic writing/English as a second language class: Melting pot or mishmash? *Journal of Basic Writing, 11*(1), 58–74.

Braine, G. (1996). ESL students in first-year writing courses: ESL versus mainstream classes. *Journal of Second Language Writing, 5,* 91–107.

Chiang, Y.-S. D., & Schmida, M. (1999). Language identity and language ownership: Linguistic conflicts of first-year university writing students. In L. Harklau, K. M. Losey, & M. Siegal (Eds.), *Generation 1.5 meets college composition: Issues in the teaching of writing to U.S.-educated learners of ESL* (pp. 81–96). Mahwah, NJ: Lawrence Erlbaum.

Fu, D. (2003). *An island of English: Teaching ESL in Chinatown.* Portsmouth, NH: Heinemann.

Hamp-Lyons, L. (Ed.) (1991). *Assessing second language writing in academic contexts.* Norwood, NJ: Ablex.

Harklau, L., Siegal, M., & Losey, K. M. (1999). Linguistically diverse students and college writing: What is equitable and appropriate? In L. Harklau, K. M. Losey, & M. Siegal (Eds.), *Generation 1.5 meets college composition: Issues in the teaching of writing to U.S.-educated learners of ESL* (pp. 1–14). Mahwah, NJ: Lawrence Erlbaum.

Harklau, L., Losey, K. M., & Siegal, M. (Eds.). (1999). *Generation 1.5 meets college composition: Issues in the teaching of writing to U.S.-educated learners of ESL.* Mahwah, NJ: Lawrence Erlbaum.

Leki, I. (1991). *Understanding ESL writers: A guide for teachers.* Portsmouth, NH: Boynton/Cook Heinemann.

———. (1999). "Pretty much I screwed up": Ill-served needs of a permanent resident. In L. Harklau, K. M. Losey, & M. Siegal (Eds.), *Generation 1.5 meets college composition: Issues in the teaching of writing to U.S.-educated learners of ESL* (pp. 17–43). Mahwah, NJ: Lawrence Erlbaum.

Matsuda, P. K. (1999). Composition studies and ESL writing: A disciplinary division of labor. *College Composition and Communication, 50*(4), 699–721.

———. (2003a). Basic writing and second language writers: Toward an inclusive definition. *Journal of Basic Writing, 22*(2), 67–89.

———. (2003b). Second language writing in the twentieth century: A situated historical perspective. In B. Kroll (Ed.), *Exploring the dynamics of second language writing* (pp. 15–34). New York: Cambridge University Press.

———. (2006). The myth of linguistic homogeneity in U.S. college composition. *College English, 68*(6), 637–651.

Matsuda, P. K., & Matsuda, A. (2008). Erasure of resident ESL writers. In M. Roberge, M. Siegal, & L. Harklau (Eds.), *Generation 1.5 in college composition: Teaching academic writing to U.S.-educated learners of ESL.* London: Routledge.

Matsuda, P. K., & Silva, T. (1999). Cross-cultural composition: Mediated integration of U.S. and international students. *Composition Studies, 27*(1), 15-30.

Reid, J. (1998). "Eye" learners and "ear" learners: Identifying the language needs of international student and U.S. resident writers. In P. Byrd & J. M. Reid (Eds.), *Grammar in the composition classroom: Essays on teaching ESL for college-bound students* (pp. 3–17). Boston: Heinle & Heinle.

Roberge, M., Siegal, M., & Harklau, L. (Eds.). (2008). *Generation 1.5 in college composition: Teaching academic writing to U.S.-educated learners of ESL*. London: Routledge.

Roy, A. M. (1984). Alliance for literacy: Teaching non-native speakers and speakers of nonstandard English together. *College Composition and Communication, 35*, 439–448.

——. (1988). ESL concerns for writing program administrators: Problems and policies. *Writing Program Administration, 11*, 17–28.

Shaughnessy, M. P. (1976). Diving in: An introduction to basic writing. *College Composition and Communication, 27*(3), 234–239.

Silva, T. (1994). An examination of writing program administrator's options for the placement of ESL students in first year writing classes. *Writing Program Administration, 18*, 37–43.

Slager, W. (1956). The foreign student and the immigrant—their different problems as students of English. *Language Learning, 6*(3/4), 24–29.

Soliday, M. (1994). Translating self and difference through literacy narratives. *College English, 56*(5), 511–526.

Valdés, G. (1992). Bilingual minorities and language issues in writing: Toward professionwide responses to a new challenge. *Written Communication, 9*(1), 85–136.

Williams, J. (1995). ESL composition program administration in the United States. *Journal of Second Language Writing, 4*(20), 157–179.

Appendix

Sample Student Interview Questions to Identify ESL Student's Language Background (Reid, 1998, pp. 8–9) ——

1. Is English your second (or third or fourth) language? _____

    - What is your first language? _____
    - List your previous schooling
      in your first language: grade _____ through grade _____

      total years _____

      in English: grade _____ through grade _____

      total years _____

2. Did you graduate from a U.S. high school?

    Yes _____   No _____

3. If the answer to the last question is

No	Yes
(*Usually* indicates an international student)	(*Usually* indicates a U.S. resident)
- TOEFL® score _____	- high school attended _____
- TOEFL® section scores:	- graduate in what year _____
Listening _____	- ESL classes taken _____ hours
Structure/Writing _____	each week in grades _____
Reading _____	to _____
- full-time English study	- was your first language school-ing interrupted?
Yes ____ No ____	Yes ____ No ____
- if yes, where?	- If yes, how long? _____
_____	- fluency in first language (high, medium, low)
how long? _____	speaking & listening _____
	reading _____
	writing _____

Sample Follow-Up Questions for ESL Student Writers ——

1. How did you learn English?	a lot	some	a little	none
• studying grammar				
• listening to English speakers				
• practicing with language tapes				
• reading English literature				
• watching U.S. movies				
• watching U.S. television				
• using computer websites				
• other: _____				

2. How would you evaluate your English language proficiency?

	excellent	very good	average	poor
• speaking				
• listening				
• reading				
• writing				
• grammar				

MYTH(S) 9

Students' Myths about Academic Writing and Teaching

Joy Reid
Maui Community College

WHEN I STARTED TEACHING IN 1966, there were virtually no teacher resource materials for teaching ESL writing, so my first years were spent asking and learning from students. That habit has become integral to my teaching philosophy. As I enter my 44th year of teaching, I continue to ask students questions, primarily because I am so far removed from their lives, but at least once a semester, I continue to inquire about their attitudes about and experiences with writing—their myths.

I have taught only one elective class in my career (Sociolinguistics, which, not surprisingly, is my favorite). Indeed, I almost never enter a classroom to greet students who want to be there, so a substantial part of my job has been to (a) dispel student myths about composition courses and (b) persuade my students that the academic writing course is worth their time and effort. For this chapter, I report on beliefs—myths—that students have about writing instruction and writing instructors, and I offer pedagogical options to help dispel those myths. I also include ways in which many of these myths are perpetuated by writing teachers.

<u>Note</u>: In contrast to the other empirically based chapters in this anthology, my chapter is based on the questions I have asked, and discussions I have had with ESL and NES composition students over the years. I present this information to encourage better understanding of some of the causes of student resistance and frustration in composition classes, and to help teachers decrease these feelings.

In the Real World

Today, I teach as a temporary, part-time person (a return to my early career) at Maui Community College, where my students include international and resident students, NESs, and, mostly, native Hawaiians and Filipino, Portuguese, Japanese, Chinese, and mixed-heritage students whose first language is Hawaiian "pidgin" (actually a Creole). Even among this diversity, their myths are similar to those I have encountered previously.

Some of these student myths are common, and teachers work to dispel them; here are five **well-known** student myths.

1. "Good writers are born. I wasn't one of them."
2. "I have nothing to say."
3. "Good essays are five paragraphs."
4. "Don't use 'I' in academic writing."
5. "Writing teachers grade subjectively."

We writing teachers often encounter examples of these common myths, and we may respond lightly: "Oh sure, I toss each set of papers down the stairs. Those that land on the first step get an A, those that landed on the second step got a B, . . . " Or we may talk briefly about how the problem isn't that students have nothing to write about, but rather that they have so much. Or perhaps we try to persuade students that everyone in the class can learn to be a better and an effective academic writer.

But such student perceptions will persist unless we accept them as serious and important issues for our students. Otherwise, these perceptions based on myth can foster resistance and even ill-will in a writing class. We must therefore be willing to make the necessary efforts to substitute truth for myth. The first step is to discover your students' attitudes and myths about writing and then to face them with the the whole class. During the early weeks of class, ask students to list the five most important "beliefs" they have about writing. Some of the myths listed will invariably appear. Make three columns on the board: **Myth, It Depends** (many grammar and sentence structure "rules" will go in this column), and **Truth**. As students share their beliefs, list each in one of the columns and collect the student lists. The results can function as topics for ongoing discussions (for which the teacher is fully prepared) about whichever myths occur on several lists.

Hidden Student Myths ——

Other student myths may not appear until later in the class, when the writing community is more comfortable, and some are more subtle, and thus more difficult to confront. Here are five, along with ways we may perpetuate the myth, and ways to teach students the truth to replace the myth.

1. the grammar myth
2. the inspiration myth
3. the every-paper-is-a-brand-new-ballgame myth
4. the inoculation myth
5. the writing-teachers-know-the-secret-of-successful academic writing, but-they-won't-tell-us myth

STUDENT MYTH 1: The Grammar Myth

"My audience will understand if my grammar is correct."

"If my grammar is right, the writing will be good."

Until the 1970s, many ESL teachers believed that actual composing and writing should be postponed until students "knew" their grammar. That is, if students concentrated on learning English grammar first, the "rest" would take care of itself. Of course, we know that effective academic writing is more complex than simply grammar. We might even say that grammar is a tool, like handwriting or spelling, that helps writers communicate their ideas effectively. At most, language structure/grammar is as important as (a) content and (b) organization. Further, we understand that research has demonstrated, since the 1960s, that grammar exercises, particularly those that are not deeply rooted in the context of the assignment, do not transfer to future student writing (despite the high comfort level students and many teachers have with such exercises).

HOW WE PERPETUATE THE GRAMMAR MYTH

- by believing, as the students do, and teaching, that grammar is the heart and soul of effective academic writing
- by marking every grammar error in student writing and commenting on every grammar mistake, with gusto, an indication of the supreme importance of grammar
- by not providing substantial skills and strategies for grammar revision, and not insisting that students make use of those strategies (Ferris & Hedgcock, 2007)

What We Can Do: Grammar Myth

1. Make sure that the only grammar taught in any EAP writing class is (a) relevant to all students, (b) directly relevant to the discourse of academic writing, and (c) relevant to the current writing assignment (Conrad, 2000).

2. Then give students multiple opportunities to investigate and practice that grammar point.

3. Mark grammar errors on student writing that are "treatable" by the students, but correct grammar errors that students will find difficult to correct. (See Myth 5, Ferris, this volume for many specifics and exercises.)

4. To demonstrate the importance of rhetoric and thought in writing, give (at least major) assignments three equally important grades: the first for organization, the next for content, and the final for language/structure.

5. Refer students to external sources, particularly writing labs or help centers available on the campus, and encourage them to discover these resources by assigning:

   - a memo describing their experience
   - a quiz based on their experience (What was the name of your tutor? What was he or she wearing? What was the first question the tutor asked?)
   - a one-minute oral report detailing one thing the student learned during the session

6. See Myth 3, Byrd and Bunting, in this volume for additional information about grammar in the composition classroom.

STUDENT MYTH 2: The Inspiration Myth

"I have to wait until an idea hits me."

"I work best when I don't start until the deadline is near."

"Good writers get it done in one draft."

One basis for this myth is the one paper the student wrote (or her best friend wrote) at the last minute in fifth grade that received praise and an A from the teacher. At best, such successes are rare; perspiration rather than inspiration is responsible for consistently effective academic writing. Another reason is that the student believes in the every-paper-is-a-brand-new-ballgame myth (see Student Myth 3). This student simply does not believe, or perhaps has not experienced, that starting early, and learning and using writing conventions, will more easily and consistently result in effective academic writing.

HOW WE PERPETUATE THE INSPIRATION MYTH

- by simply assigning the paper and assigning the final grade
- by allowing students to wait until the last moment to write anything

---

What We Can Do: Inspiration Myth

1. Support students in their belief (not a myth) that writing is complex and time-consuming, that the field of composition and rhetoric is one that is studied by those seeking advanced degrees, and that perspiration reigns, even for professional writers.

   Read aloud what authors of fiction have to say about composing. Then send students out for an additional opinion by assigning them to interview (carefully selected, articulate) disciplinary professors who publish.

Sample Interview Questions:

- What is the hardest part about writing for publication?
- Do you do research before or as you write? If so, how and how much?
- Do you revise as you write or after you write a draft? If so, how and how often?
- How long does it take you to write an article for a refereed journal?
- How many drafts and revisions do you do for most of your articles?
- Do you write differently, depending on which journal you will submit your article to? If so, how?
- How do you respond to reviewers' comments on your submission? For example, do you revise exactly, according to the comments, or do you revise just those parts that you believe need revision?

2. **Demonstrate, for every piece of writing you assign, the complicated interactive and recursive processes, the hundreds of decisions, that characterize successful academic writing.**

- Set a timeline for the assignment, with something due every day.
  —Require (and give credit for) **gathering processes:**

    ‣ two forms of prewriting
    ‣ several development exercises (e.g., an essay map, a list of end-of-text references, a list of supporting examples and details for one body paragraph).

- Include daily deadlines and in-class work that are directly related to the assignment, working specifically with **selecting processes.**
  —Work with student thesis statements on the chalkboard
  —Student pairs exchange essay maps, and ask questions

they expect to be answered in each body paragraph; the teacher has mini-conferences and checks homework.

- Require that "pieces" of the paper be read by audiences, working specifically with audience and purpose issues as they are related to **presenting processes.**
    —Plan peer response exercises, in pairs and in small groups, as the teacher mini-conferences and checks homework.
    —Pick up one to two pieces of student work for each paper (e.g., just the introductory paragraph, or just one body paragraph).

- Insist on the importance of revision, during drafting and after the "final" draft is turned in, marked, and returned. Because students learn as much about writing from revision as they do from originally writing a paper, award revisions an additional grade (for the grading suggested above, a fourth grade for revision, so that a complete revision is worth 25 percent of the assignment's grade).

STUDENT MYTH 3: The Every-Paper-Is-a-Brand-New-Ballgame Myth

Many students firmly believe that each assigned academic paper is a completely new, never-before-conceived, what-does-this-teacher-want task. However, an important fact students must learn is that some writing conventions are transferable from one paper and even one discipline to another. Students therefore need to be taught and persuaded that academic writing, like other disciplines such as math, biology, or psychology, have rules, even formulas (what English teachers call *conventions*). Further, they need to recognize which conventions can be transferred and/or adapted to any assigned academic writing task.

HOW WE PERPETUATE THE EVERY-PAPER-IS-A-BRAND-NEW-BALLGAME MYTH

- by not differentiating between transferable and non-transferable strategies
- by assigning papers, such as personal narratives or movie reviews, whose conventions are not easily transferable to academic writing

---

What We Can Do: Every-Paper-Is-a-Brand-New-Ballgame Myth

1. **Investigate and then teach students about transferable and non-transferable conventions.** (See Myth 5, Ferris, in this volume for specific information.)

    - Academic writing conventions are similar, even exact, regardless of the assignment:
        —the overall organization, the analysis of the audience processes
        —the functions (if not the length) of an introduction or a conclusion
        —the general-to-specific organization of many body paragraphs
        —the frequent use of *to be* and *to have.*

    - Some conventions are similar and adaptable:
        —the frequency and choice of transitions, report verbs, and noun phrases
        —the amount and kind of specific supporting detail in body paragraphs
        —the use of definition conventions.

    - Other writing conventions may be new to the writer:
        —the use of author and article name, and a single point from the article, at the beginning of body paragraphs in a summary-response
        —the differences between personal narrative and historical narrative conventions

—the reasons for use of passive voice in scientific and newspaper writing

2. **Provide students with authentic examples of transferable and non-transferable writing conventions.**

   - Start with the most obvious: the overall organization of almost all academic writing, from doctoral theses to anatomy experimental reports to even literary analysis:
     —The introduction: a general beginning about the specific topic that is non-controversial (usually one sentence in two- to four-page papers, perhaps a paragraph or two in graduate theses). This introductory sentence is followed by a sentence or two (in two- to four-page papers) about the topic that will interest—"hook"—reader. Finally, the introduction ends with the thesis statement, the most general, most important sentence in the essay.
     —The background paragraph (called *methods* and/or *materials* in most scientific reports, but *background* in most academic papers): Information about the specific topic necessary for the reader to continue—for example, a history of a controversy, definitions of terms, a description of a process involved in the content of the paper such as an interview or a survey (Reid, 2006).
     —The conclusion: may include a combination of summary, recommendations, predictions, or solutions.

3. See Myth 1, Folse, in this volume for authentic examples and exercises for psychology vocabulary.

4. See Myth 6, Conrad, in this volume for work with authentic examples and exercises for biology and history grammar and lexical conventions.

STUDENT MYTH 4: The Inoculation Myth

"I've always been a good writer. My teachers loved my writing."

"Everything I needed to know about writing I learned before eighth grade."

"So why am I stuck in another writing class?"

Math curricula do a better job than English curricula. One year, students learn addition; another year, their multiplication tables; still another year, geometry; eventually they may learn calculus. There is not much overlap: The skills and terminology for calculus are "saved" for that class. But in composition:

- Pre-school students dictate stories to teachers-on-keyboards.
- Third graders write letters to the editor.
- Fifth graders write "research" papers.
- Eighth graders write two-page mystery novels and plays.

In fact, by secondary school, students merely yawn at the mention of thesis statements, "hamburger paragraphs" and five-paragraph themes. No wonder so many students feel they have been completely "inoculated" about writing, and thus enter first-year composition jaded. Often, these students write every college writing assignment the same way—the way they learned "before."

HOW WE PERPETUATE THE INOCULATION MYTH

- by assuming that students "know" how to write (and if they don't, "they shouldn't be in college"—otherwise called the elitist myth)
- by failing to persuade students that successful academic writing includes
  —multiple skills and strategies, determining audience and purpose, which is complicated and time-consuming

—knowledge of genre and rhetorical conventions, which is real and essential to practice for effective academic writing
- by not making evaluation and grading processes transparent

What We Can Do: Inoculation Myth

1. **Begin the class by discovering what students really know by offering the most innovative assignments first.**
   For instance, work deeply with an assignment, with multiple tasks and various products that will demonstrate skills students need to practice. Analyze content, organization, language; spending time with each assignment demonstrates the complexity of writing processes. Each of these extensive exercises can be adapted for any level of writing proficiency.

   - Ask students to analyze the target audience of a magazine they choose to bring to class (age, education, interests, socioeconomic status, etc.); ask them to investigate how advertisers select magazines for their products; ask them to discover how much magazine (and other media) advertising costs; branch out into discussing and researching how marketing products influences our lives. Students can learn to write a paragraph describing the attributes of a magazine ad, an analytic report using data collected from the magazine that support their analysis of target audience; they can learn to read and then perhaps make such non-text materials as the tables of advertising costs, using or perhaps developing and using a survey to discover what others know about advertising or target audiences; they might write a letter to an advertiser or design a full-page advertisement and then write or orally report on their processes.

   - Plan a series of writing assignments around the campus that provides students with authentic and relevant information as well as challenges them to write clear prose for a specific audience: ask students to investigate clubs, odd buildings, the registration process, the online course/teacher evaluation results, the literary magazine or newspaper, the special programs (Head Start? Dinosaur Museum? Culinary Program?). Work to develop processes, interview questions, interviewees (and etiquette); have students use the college homepage, the local newspaper, every brochure they can pick up. Students might make or adapt maps, summarize program brochures, learn to use interview/direct reporting information, analyze the effectiveness of the library or the learning center, or find out about cutting edge technology or research. Skills and strategies discussed and practiced can include note-taking, memo-writing, summarizing, paraphrasing, and, throughout, a focus on audience and purpose. Students might then publish their articles in the school newspaper, create a website for incoming new students, or develop a brochure for a campus club.

2. **Teach the relatively complex processes involved in evaluating academic writing.**

   For instance, we can develop and then carefully teach—with specific examples—the grading rubric we use for student papers. Of course, we must then use the rubric and make it apparent that we have used that rubric by, perhaps, clear end comments, a cover sheet with the rubric and places for us to write, and full class discussion about the application of the rubric.

   Begin by making sure students understand each evaluation criterion. Explain any terms, and indicate the value of each criterion in your grading system. For instance, *coherence* is a difficult term; further, its meanings differ in the *Wall Street Journal*, a short story, a grant proposal, and an academic essay.

Exercises:

- Help students experience criteria development by bringing three different brands of a food product to class (e.g., potato chips, chocolate chip cookies, hard candy). In small groups, ask students to negotiate the four criteria (besides the basic criterion, price per serving) on which to base their evaluation of the three brands. As students report those criteria, indicate which are too abstract (e.g., appearance) or too broad (e.g., taste) and ways these criteria must be made more specific. Then ask students to complete an analysis form, using 1–5 stars (*) to evaluate each brand. Finally, have each group make recommendations of one brand for three groups of people (e.g., grandparents, children, college students), and explain why, based on their criteria. Finally, link such criteria development to criteria used in evaluation of student papers.
- Discuss with students four or five criteria used to evaluate their writing. Providing samples of student writing (from classes at least a year previous), both well-written and ineffectively written, will help students clearly define and understand evaluation expectations in the writing class.

  —Give students a hard copy of evaluation criteria.

  —Use a form of that copy as a grading sheet.
- At advanced levels of writing proficiency, and about mid-semester, asking students to help devise additional or alternative criteria often results in more clarity.

3. **It is probably too late to revolutionize elementary and secondary school English curricula to parallel the math route. However, we can slow down the writing process in our ESL writing programs, not by singling out skills for each level, but by determining the ease and difficulty of various skills and then spiraling writing strategies and skills that are**

complex and time-consuming through a several-level program (Reid, 2000).

Examples

- Audience awareness is often a new and difficult concept. Developmentally, traditionally aged students have only rarely had to think beyond themselves. (See Myth 7, Cavusgil, in this volume for additional exercises.)

Sample Exercise

—At <u>lower levels</u> of writing proficiency, students focus on identifying and analyzing excerpts about the same topic from (a) a children's book, (b) a secondary school textbook, and (c) a scientific journal article.

—<u>Intermediate</u> students practice summarizing longer but similar excerpts, perhaps working in pairs, and then discuss the differences in language and the problems in finding synonyms for their summaries.

—<u>Advanced</u> students read (a) popular articles and (b) original journal articles about scientific research and perform a data analysis on 350 words of each.

- Because academic research and citation conventions are so complicated, they should be taught in every level of a writing program (See Myth 2, Schuemann, in this volume).

Sample Exercise

—<u>Lower levels</u>: students identify a celebrity and access information about that person on the Internet (using Google™) and print two short articles. Then students list the title, author, and Internet source; write three main ideas in each article; and report those six ideas orally to the class about the celebrity.

—<u>Intermediate levels</u>: Students select a question from a list and investigate the answers to the questions by gathering information—three or four articles—on the Internet (using Google™). Students practice summary writing for each article, and they learn the basic conventions for for in-text and end-of-text academic citations for those articles. Students prepare for a two-minute oral report that answers the question by writing a formal outline of the talk, writing a Reference page, and developing an interactive exercise or handout for their classmates

Sample Questions:

- ▸ What is/are (autism, the Night Walkers, the Doll Test)?
- ▸ How does/do (a water tower, a jet stream, steroids) work?
- ▸ Why is/are (microexpressions, endorphins, *feng shui*) important?

—<u>Advanced</u>: Students select a small local "problem" that irritates them, that can be solved, and for which there is an available "authority" to interview. They use the internet, surveys, and interviews to propose a solution to the problem, and their report contains five to eight in-text and end-of-text citations as well as two to three examples of nontext materials (tables, figures, illustrations). A copy of the revised paper is sent to the original interviewee with a cover letter.

- Have students plan, but not write, two to three writing assignments throughout the course. Included can be planning forms, ranging from processes like narrowing the topic to selecting the focus, from audience analysis to essay map, from research notes to organization processes, from listing general and specific details to listing concluding techniques to be used. Working on these processes slows down students' writing and shows them how much work experienced writers do even before they write a first draft. At the end of the semester, ask students to include one of the papers, fully written, as one of their portfolio documents.

- Construct a broad, disciplinary-based academic vocabulary strand throughout the writing curriculum (Folse, 2004, 2006; Nation, 2001).

STUDENT MYTH 5: The Writing-Teachers-Know-the-Secrets-of-Successful-Academic-Writing, But They-Won't-Tell-Us Myth

"I just turn in papers and hope for the best."

"If I knew what [this teacher] wanted, I could get an easy A."

"I got an A on this same paper in my (biology, history, art) class."

"Here's the game [the teacher] plays: After we write the paper and get a grade, [he or she] shows us what we should have done."

This is the deepest-seated myth that writing students have, and sometimes students don't even recognize the belief until another student mentions it. It is also the most difficult myth to overcome because, in some ways, the perception springs from the reality of other college courses.

That is, in most other classes (biology, history, psychology), students usually know where they stand and what to expect. If they read and understand the textbook, listen to and take good notes on the lectures, and answer test questions appropriately, they can be assured of a relatively high course grade. For written assignments in such courses, students know they must demonstrate that they understand the **content** of the course, from correct math formulas to analysis of an engineering problem to a sociology definition. (Note that content knowledge does not necessarily include writing skills or conventions.)

But writing classes, particularly those in which the students are expected to "express" themselves, to "cultivate" their own "voices," can seem to students to be a crap shoot. After all, they know the basics— the five-paragraph structure, the thesis statement, the use of transitions—so what's wrong with the papers they turn in? Why aren't they successful? And why, when they follow the teacher's advice, do they always make more mistakes and get more advice? If they read the textbook (the content of the course) and take notes in class, why aren't their papers effective? Why can't the teacher simply tell them what he or she *wants*? This question is neither insulting nor personal: It is a plea for the clarity students find in other classes. Further, for ESL students, the problems multiply because their depth of cultural and contextual knowledge needed for effective academic writing is limited (Angelova & Riazantseva, 1999).

This myth is like an "umbrella" that underlies all others. For example, students can only guess how to write successful papers because the grades seem so arbitrarily assigned; why not just wait until the last minute and hope it works? Why, if the paper doesn't have any grammar mistakes and it has five paragraphs, isn't it a good paper (especially if grammar is clearly the focus of the class)? And if grading is so subjective, then every writing assignment *is* a brand-new ballgame— except for those students who already seem to know the secrets of effective academic writing. Consider the students' images associated with this myth: Writing teachers whipping off a novel one week, an article the next, in one draft apiece, then laughing with other colleagues about student errors. And then consider the risk of bringing our own writing to class, draft after draft, self-marked and ready for yet another revision: Might we be some of the few writing teachers who don't even know the secret? Yikes!

HOW WE PERPETUATE THE WRITING-TEACHERS-KNOW-THE-SECRETS-OF-SUCCESSFUL-ACADEMIC-WRITING, BUT THEY-WON'T-TELL-US MYTH

- by assigning no student grades until the end of the course
- by assuring students that grades aren't important
- by not telling the students what we "want"
- by insisting that students "discover" their academic "voices"
- by not giving students clear parameters for writing evaluation, or
- by not valuing the grading criteria

What We Can Do: Writing-Teachers-Know-the-Secrets Myth

1. **Demonstrate without qualification how hard writing is.**
   Using effective and less effective writing samples, teach students how to analyze problems: Which composing decisions did this writer not make, or make incorrectly? Start with extremely poor writing samples (without student writers' names, and not samples from recent classes) so students can notice the problems themselves (but save grammar problems until late in the course, if at all—students already know how language errors can "ruin" writing).

2. **Begin even with lower levels of writing proficiency, to teach genre** (*cf.* Henry & Roseberry, 1998; Hyland, 2004; Hyon, 1996; Johns, 2002).

   Exercises:

   - Use substantial in-class time analyzing text, from vocabulary words to discipline-specific sentence structures.
     —At <u>lower levels</u> of writing proficiency, spend time identifying and analyzing differences between spoken and

written English (Biber, Conrad, Reppen, Byrd, & Helt, 2002; Biber, 2006). Then have students investigate and work with Coxhead's Academic Word List (AWL) (2000) on the Internet (see Myth 3, Byrd and Bunting, in this volume for activities).

—At the <u>intermediate level</u>, students can study differences between popular writing and academic writing. Use popular magazines and/or romantic novels, student papers from general education courses and/or excerpts from Master's theses, and construct brief pair or small group exercises: In a sample of 300 words (selected from the body of each sample), count the number of verbs (divide into modal verbs, verbs *to be* and *to have*, and passive voice verbs); calculate (a) average word length, (b) average sentence length, and (c) average paragraph length.

—As students <u>advance</u> in proficiency, they can identify and analyze differences among disciplinary language and structures (*cf.* Biber, 2006; Conrad, 2001; Stoller, Jones, Costanza-Robinson, & Robinson, 2005).

• Ask students to locate (a) information about writing memos and (b) a template for memos on the Internet. Discuss what conventions are involved in writing a memo. Analyze several memos for those conventions (start with poorly written memos, perhaps from the college).

• Incorporate transferable and discipline-specific vocabulary study into every assignment (see Myth 1, Folse, in this volume).

• Discuss some of what researchers have found about writing conventions in different academic disciplines (Byrd, 1988; Carter, 2004; Conrad, 1996, 2001; Hyland & Bondi, 2006).

Examples

—A major geology journal uses exclamation points occasionally.

—The new trend in some major science journals is to eliminate passive voice.

—The use of "hedges" in various disciplines (see Myth 4, Hyland, in this volume).

3. **Become familiar with corpus analysis processes** (Tardy, 2006). **Introduce corpus analysis on the Internet, and involve students in discourse analysis.** (Gaskell & Cobb, 2004; Yoon & Hirvela, 2004).

   - At the intermediate level, show how corpus analysis and discourse analysis "work," (see Myth 6, Conrad, in this volume for specifics) and work through several appropriately difficult samples.
   - Ask students to perform small corpus analyses (see Myth 6, Conrad, in this volume for exercises).

4. **Finally, assign relevant, authentic academic writing assignments. Begin by designing an assignment that students can succeed with.**

   That is, provide enough information about your expectations: clear instructions, advice about using effective conventions, and topics carefully pre-tested for success (Reid & Kroll, 1995).

   Poor Examples

   - Life. Discuss.
   - Choose a topic from the index of our textbook.

5. **Understand how important grades are for students.**

   Ease their anxiety by not teasing them with secret-code grades, and support their need to know. In addition, make absolutely clear how they can improve their grades.

- Have clear grading policies available to students, in writing, the first day of class. Discuss fully. Students should know their current grade at any point during the class, even without consulting the teacher.
- Directly link the grading processes for student writing with designed and explained criteria (see Student Myth 4, the Inoculation Myth).
- Explain ways of raising a student's grade by, for example, spending quality time on revising, completing the exercises preceding the papers, etc.

All myths begin with a seed of truth; writing myths are no exception. Yet often the more experienced the teacher, the less often we remember that students bring their myths with them to composition classes. Just as we check—with each of our classes—to determine what our students know about academic writing, so we discover what we should review and what we must teach, we need also to surprise our students by discussing the differences between writing myths and truths. Many students are not fully aware of these beliefs—some may never have analyzed their negative feelings about writing classes. If they can be persuaded to recognize and analyze their myths, they will begin to believe that effective academic writing is worthwhile and within their reach.

Teaching is learning (else how could we stand to teach?). We continue to ask questions, of colleagues, experts . . . and students. As we discuss students' writing myths, we may learn as much as we teach. For instance, during a recent discussion of myths with my students, I discovered that (a) most students no longer wear watches (they use their cell phones), (b) most students (and younger teachers) no longer write in cursive, and many students cannot read cursive teacher-comments, and (c) many students no longer use email (instead, they use text- and instant-messaging); thus, assignments that ask students to engage in discussions in class chat/discussion scenarios are considered old fashioned and busy work.

As students become aware of writing myths and writing conventions, their attitudes toward academic writing often change. As they realize that even experienced and professional writers find that writing takes time, patience, and thought, they become more willing to identify, analyze, and practice various gathering, selecting, and presenting processes. As they open to the possibility that they still can learn skills and strategies that will improve their writing, they are surprised.

Questions for Reflection

1. Did any of the student myths described in this chapter surprise you? Which of them do you think causes student resistance in the classroom? Do you believe that teachers perpetuate these myths?

2. What other student myths about writing have you encountered? How do teachers perpetuate those myths, and how can we help to dispel and replace those myths?

3. Many of the chapters in this book recommend that ESL/EFL writing teachers focus on teaching students to take time to write. What techniques, in this book and in your repertoire, do you find helpful in achieving this goal?

4. Identify the writing tasks and skills completed by students in a course you teach. Explain how some of those tasks and skills are transferable to other courses. What actions do/can you take to assure that students are aware of this transfer of skills?

5. Like several other chapters in this book, the focus of this chapter includes ESL writing curricula that begin academic research and citation even at the lower levels of language proficiency. What are the advantages and disadvantage of such a curricular change? Do you think that this decision is viable?

References

Angelova, M., & Riazantseva, A. (1999). "If you don't tell me, how can I know?" A case study of four international students learning to write the U.S. way. *Written Communication 16*, 491–525.

Biber, D. (2006). *University language*. Amsterdam: John Benjamins.

Biber, D., Conrad, S., Reppen, R., Byrd, P., & Helt, M. (2002). Speaking and writing in the university: A multidimensional comparison. *TESOL Quarterly, 36*(1), 9–48.

Byrd, P. (1998). Grammar in the composition syllabus. In P. Byrd & J. Reid (Eds.), *Grammar in the composition classroom* (pp. 33–53). Boston: Heinle & Heinle.

Carter, R. (2004). Grammar and spoken English. In C. Coffin, A. Hewings, & K. O'Halloran (Eds.), *Applying English grammar: Functional and corpus approaches* (pp. 25–39). London: Hodder Arnold.

Conrad, S. (1996). Investigating academic texts with corpus-based techniques: An example from biology. *Linguistics and Education, 8*, 299–326.

———. (2000). Will corpus linguistics revolutionize grammar teaching in the 21st century? *TESOL Quarterly, 34*(3), 548–559.

———. (2001). Variation among disciplinary texts: A comparison of textbooks and journal articles in biology and history. In S. Conrad & D. Biber (Eds.), *Multi-dimensional studies of register variation in English* (pp. 94–107). Harlow, UK: Pearson Education.

Coxhead, A. (2000). A new academic word list. *TESOL Quarterly, 34*(2), 213–238.

Ferris, D., & Hedgcock, J. (2007). *Teaching ESL composition: Purpose, process, & practice* (2nd ed.). Mahwah NJ: Lawrence Erlbaum.

Folse, K. (2004). *Vocabulary myths: Applying second language research to classroom teaching*. Ann Arbor: University of Michigan Press.

———. (2006). The effect of type of written exercise on L2 vocabulary retention. *TESOL Quarterly, 40*(2), 273–293.

Gaskell, D., & Cobb, T. (2004). Can learners use concordancer feedback for writing errors? *System, 32*, 301–319.

Henry, A., & Roseberry, R. L. (1998). An evaluation of a genre-based approach to the teaching of EAP/ESP writing. *TESOL Quarterly, 32*, 147–156.

Hyland, K. (2004). *Genre and second language writing*. Ann Arbor: University of Michigan Press.

Hyland, K., & Bondi, M. (Eds.). (2006). *Academic discourse across disciplines.* Oxford, UK: Peter Lang.

Hyon, S. (1996). Genre in three traditions: Implications for ESL. *TESOL Quarterly, 30,* 693-722.

Johns, A. M. (2002). *Genre in the classroom: Multiple perspectives.* Mahwah, NJ: Lawrence Erlbaum.

Nation, P. (2001). *Learning vocabulary in another language.* Cambridge, UK: Cambridge University Press.

Reid, J. (2000). Advanced EAP writing and curriculum design: What do we need to know? In *On second language writing: Proceedings of the symposium on second language writing, Purdue University, (September, 1998)* (pp. 143–160). Mahwah, NJ: Lawrence Erlbaum.

Reid, J. (2006). *Essentials of teaching academic writing.* Boston: Heinle & Heinle.

Reid, J. & Kroll, B. (1995). Designing and assessing effective classroom writing assignments, *Journal of Second Language Writing, 4*(1), 17–41.

Stoller, F., Jones, J., Costanza-Robinson, M., & Robinson, M. (2005). Demystifying disciplinary writing: A case study in the writing of chemistry. *Across the disciplines: Interdisciplinary perspectives on language, learning and academic writing, 2.* Retrieved March 6, 2007, from http://wac.colostate.eduatd/lds/ stoller.cfm

Tardy, C. M. (2006). Research first and second language genre learning: A comparative review and a look ahead. *Journal of Second Language Writing 15*(2), 79–101.

Yoon, H., & Hirvela, A. (2004). ESL student attitudes towards corpus use in L2 writing. *Journal of Second Language Writing, 13,* 257–283.

Author Biodata

John Bunting is a senior lecturer in the Intensive English Program and the Department of Applied Linguistics and ESL at Georgia State University. He has taught EFL in Venezuela and has presented at conferences in the United States, Mexico, Peru, and the Dominican Republic. His interests include the use of corpus linguistics in language teaching and learning, L2 vocabulary development, technology in the language classroom, and assessment.

Pat Byrd is a recently retired professor in the Department of Applied Linguistics & ESL at Georgia State University in Atlanta. She continues to teach graduate courses in English grammar, corpus linguistics, phraseology, and CALL. Her publications include research on English grammar in various discourse settings along with classroom teaching materials, the most recent of which is the series of EAP textbooks coedited with Joy Reid and Cynthia Schuemann.

Sharon Cavusgil is a lecturer in the Department of Applied Linguistics & ESL at Georgia State University where she has taught in the Intensive English Program, ESL credit program, and master's program. She serves as coordinator of ESL graduate and undergraduate courses and works with the university's College of Education to coordinate ESOL efforts across numerous metro-Atlanta public schools. She has published textbooks in the areas of academic writing and content-based instruction.

Susan Conrad is professor of Applied Linguistics at Portland State University. She has taught ESL/EFL writing in South Korea, southern Africa, and the United States. She is coauthor of the *Longman Grammar of Spoken and Written English* and *Corpus Linguistics: Investigating Language Structure and Use* and has published numerous articles on applying corpus linguistics to the study of English grammar and writing.

Dana Ferris is a professor of English at California State University–Sacramento where she coordinates the multilingual writing program and teaches TESOL and applied linguistics courses. She is the author or coauthor of a number of books, chapters, and articles on second language writing, including *Treatment of Error in Second Language Writing Classes* (University of Michigan Press, 2002), *Teaching ESL Composition* (with John Hedgcock, Erlbaum, 2005), and forthcoming books on teaching second language readers (also with John Hedgcock) and on including three different student audiences in college-level instruction.

Keith S. Folse is associate professor of TESOL and coordinates the MATESOL program at the University of Central Florida. He has received several teaching, research, and scholarly awards and is the author of more than 40 books, including *Vocabulary Myths* and *The Art of Teaching Speaking* (University of Michigan Press, 2002, 2006) and *Greater Essays* (Heinle/Cengage). He is a frequent conference presenter on best practices in teaching vocabulary, grammar, composition, reading, and speaking.

Ken Hyland is professor of Education and Head of the Centre for Academic and Professional Literacies at the Institute of Education, University of London. He has considerable experience teaching and researching first and second language writing and has published more than 100 articles and 10 books on writing and applied linguistics. His more recent titles are: *Teaching and Researching Writing* (Longman, 2002), *Second Language Writing* (Cambridge University Press, 2003), *Genre and Second Language Writing* (University of Michigan Press, 2004), *Metadiscourse* (Continuum, 2005), and *English for Academic Purposes* (Routledge, 2006).

Paul Kei Matsuda is an associate professor of English at Arizona State University where he works with graduate students in the Ph.D. program in Rhetoric, Composition, and Applied Linguistics as well as MA programs in TESOL and Linguistics. Founding chair of the Symposium on Second Language Writing and the CCCC Committee on Second

Language writing, he has coedited a number of books on second language writing, including *Landmark Essays on ESL Writing* (Erlbaum, 2001), *On Second Language Writing* (Erlbaum, 2001), *Second Language Writing Research* (Erlbaum, 2005), *Second Language Writing in the Composition Classroom* (Bedford/St. Martin's and NCTE, 2006), and *The Politics of Second Language Writing: In Search of the Promised Land* (Parlor Press, 2006).

Joy Reid is a retired professor from the University of Wyoming where she taught composition, ESL methods, and linguistics. She has written ESL writing textbooks and teacher resource books, and she coedited two ESL series, the most recent *English for Academic Success* (Heinle/Cengage, 2006). Her research and publication interests also include discourse analysis, learning styles, classroom change processes, and teacher preparation. Currently she teaches composition part-time at Maui Community College, a return to her early ESL career.

Cynthia M. Schuemann is a faculty member at Miami Dade College where she teaches ESL and linguistics courses. She has been with the college for more than 16 years, also serving as department chairperson. Additional teaching experiences have included assignments in Wisconsin, Arizona, Spain, and China. She is a regular presenter at local and international conferences and has also conducted teacher training workshops in Brazil and Ecuador. She has authored textbooks and articles for publication, including the coedited *English for Academic Success* series for Heinle/Cengage. She contributes to the profession as Treasurer for Sunshine State TESOL, as a board member for Miami-Dade TESOL, as past co-chair of the Materials Writers Interest Section of TESOL, and as a member of the Florida Community College EAP Consortium.

Index

academic language, written, 60–61; corpus studies of, 50–59; definition of, 47; grammar of, 47, 50, 53, 56–57; vocabulary in, 61. *See also* conventions; discourse

Academic Word List (AWL), 9, 10, 37, 44; explanation of, 60–61

analytic scoring, 7

attribution, 19, 145

audience, 100–101, 191; exercises, 85

CANCODE (Cambridge and Nottingham Corpus of Discourse of English), 53–54, 58

citation, 19–20; definition of, 22; exercises, 32–35, 38; research in, 21

collocation, 11–13; definition of, 12; and vocabulary notebook, 11–12

concordances, 73–74; exercises, 87–88; using, 87, 135

conventions, writing, for citation, 27, rhetorical 183–184, 188

corpus/corpora, 117; definition of, 49

corpus-based dictionaries, 63–64

corpus studies, 50–55, 57–58, 61–62; 74–75, 80; use of, 61–62, 126. *See also* discourse analysis

curriculum, writing, 64–65, 128–130, 187, 190–191 ; and citation, 19, 31–32, 38; and genre, 195–196; and hedging, 81; and vocabulary, 9, 14–15

deixis, 59

discourse, 45; exercises, 87–88, 130–132, 195–196

discourse analysis, 50–56, 57–58, 61–62; 74–75, 80; exercises, 195–196

editing strategies, student, 100–102; exercises, 102–103; log, 106–107

email etiquette, 141, 152

English as a second language. *See* ESL

error, ESL written, 93; exercises, 101–103; logs, 106–107, and NES error, 93–94; research in, 95; and second language acquisition, 92–93; and verbs, 61–62, 112–114. *See* also error feedback error feedback, 94–95; teacher-based, 104–106

ESL, 92–93; and error, 93–95; and international students, 161–162; and resident students, 160–162

evaluation, 7; analytic, 7; and grading, 189–190, 194, 197–198; holistic, 6, 8. *See* also writing

feedback. *See* error feedback

General Service List, 60

genre, 195–196

glue words, 29

grammar, and academic prose, 47, 50, 53, 55–57; exercises, 66, 67; instruction, 108–109, 177; research in, 50–56, 57–58; and vocabulary, 47–48

grammar reference books, 50–51, 53–54, 63–66, 127

hedges, 70–71; exercises, 81–83; most frequently used, 71; reasons for use, 76–78, 124–125; research in, 84; research methods for, 73–74; strength of, 75. *See also* stance

holistic scoring, 6, 8

identification writing tasks, 147, 149; exercises, 153–155

idiolect, 30

immigrant ESL students. *See* resident ESL students

international ESL students, 161–162

interview exercises, student, 125, 183–184

L2. *See* ESL

Lancaster-Oslo-Bergen Corpus of British English (LOB), 50

language variation, 55–57; definition of, 116

lexical chunks. *See* lexical bundles

lexical bundles, 14, 57–58; definition of, 57, 124; exercises, 135; for hedging, 134; use of, 123–125; used in history and biology writing, 57

lexical verbs. *See* verbs, lexical

London-Lund Corpus of Spoken English, 50

Longman Spoken and Written English, 51, 120

MICASE, 45

native English speakers. *See* NES

NES, definition of, 26; and NNS error, 93–94

non-native speakers. *See* NNS

NNS, 93–94; definition of, 3

paraphrase, 2; exercises, 32, 37–38; teacher response to, 23–24

plagiarism, 1–2; and cultural

differences, 20, 24–26;
definition of, 21–22; exercises,
38–39; and vocabulary, 14
portfolios, 97–98

reference grammar books. *See*
grammar reference books
register. *See* language variation
resident ESL students, 160–162;
identifying, 166–167; needs of,
168–169; and placement,
164–165, 175–176
report verbs, 29; exercises, 36–37,
66
rubics, 5, 7–8

SLA. *See* second language
acquisition
second language acquisition,
92–93; and error, 93–94;
research in, 95
short-answer writing tasks,
148–149; exercises, 153–154
spiraling skills, 27–28, 32, 38, 39,
83–84, 169, 190–192,
195–197
spoken language, 58–60; research
in, 58–60. *See also* written vs.
spoken English
stance, 53, 58, 124. *See also*
hedges

summary, 2, 142; and vocabulary,
24–25; exercises, 32
synthesis, 2, 142

transferable writing skills,
150–153, 185–186
treatable vs. non-treatable error
types, 102; exercises, 102–104

University Word List, 9, 10. *See
also* Academic Word List

verbs, 42–43; exercises, 130–132;
lexical, 43, 57, 80–81; passive
voice, 42, 48; past/present
tense, 48–49; and persuasive
writing, 119–121; strength of
modals, 79; tense errors, 61–62
Viking Corpus of Student
Academic Writing (Portland
State), 120, 136
vocabulary notebook, 11–12

writing, ESL, 45; evaluation of,
6–7, 189–190, 194, 197–198;
taking time for, 96, 98–99,
183–184
written vs. spoken English,
53–57, 118–119, 125; and
exercises, 195–196; grammar
of, 47, 53–55, 58–60. *See also*
spoken language